TESTIMONIALS

"Great read! I learned a lot from this book. My key takeaway is to write a list of things I look for in my perfect job. I want to take ownership of my career."
Vaitheki Tharmaratnam, Management Consulting Professional

"I did not expect when I met with Marc for career counselling that I would be blown away by his commitment to his clients and helping them find the perfect job! I am inspired!"
Virginia Marshall, Technology Management Professional

"Marc Belaiche is an OUTSTANDING keynote speaker! Marc delivered a powerful and first-rate presentation on 'Social Networking Trends in the Labour Market'. The attentive capacity crowd thoroughly enjoyed his informative and very useful seminar, which received great praise."
Phil Russo, CGA, President & Director
The Canadian Institute of Management – Toronto Branch

"Marc is a true professional. I have had the privilege of working with Marc since 2009 on many occasions. His knowledge of the accounting/finance sector is beyond impressive, and it gives me great comfort to know that he represents both of our clients with professionalism, ethics, and integrity."
John Toufankjian, President & CEO, Axodis Staffing Solutions Inc.

"Through the years I have worked with Marc as well as used his services at TorontoJobs.ca. I have always found Marc to be personable, knowledgeable and to offer suggestions in order to make the services he provides a great success. Marc has wonderful creative insight and knowledge of many different things and he is always willing and open to brainstorming. Marc is an asset to any firm as he is one of the few that takes the time to talk to clients and still provides customer service regardless of the role he is in."
Lisa Maxam, Director, The Staff Room

"In my dealings with Marc he is a passionate and competent business leader with an exceptional flair for entrepreneurial success by helping his clients reduce new personnel acquisition and turnover costs. Marc has solid business acumen and is a focused and skilled leader."
Jason Stangroom, Strategic Business Advisor,
Revenue First Group Inc.

"Marc is a dynamic professional with incredible networking and personal skills. A true communicator that understands business fundamentals, you can always count on Marc for integrity and honesty."
Julie Bond, President, Bond Consulting Group

"I attended one of Marc's job fairs and one terrific way to describe it was 'bustling'. Employer booths filled the ground floor while on the second floor, career specialists helped job candidates one-on-one with their resumes. It was my first career fair and as an observer and colleague, I was impressed with the setup, range of employers, the advice being given to participants who also attended for free, and in general, the warm, congenial environment. Bravo Marc for running a much-needed service in our fair city."
Vera N. Held, President/Owner, VNH Communications

"Marc has brought out his rich experience as a recruiter in an easy-to-read story-telling format which resonates with job seekers of all kinds. He has made specific emphasis to global talent and the 'New Canadian' talent pool and provided guidelines for their successful transition to the Canadian workplace. This book is a journal which appeals to all job seekers."
Denny George, Human Resources Consultant

"As a proud Canadian, I am actually an internationally educated professional who has been fortunate to live and work in several countries. I have gained expertise in professional education and have worked with several multinational companies in the field of executive training and development. Since I returned to Canada, I have been able to assess and understand the complex and fast-paced labour market that all Canadian job seekers face and I understand that you need the right tools, resources, skills and competencies to get ahead.

I recently had the privilege and opportunity to review the draft edition of this book. In its pages, I found a great deal of advice and information. I see this book as a perfect source of key tips to help anyone successfully establish a professional career and life in Canada.

Chris the Recruiter is particularly helpful to those who face barriers to employment, lack sufficient skills and experience, and to those who need to further develop their abilities in order to make a successful transition into the Canadian labour market.

Since Canadian businesses - who employ a diverse staff - share certain characteristics, their workplaces tend to be respectful, stable, productive, innovative and energized. That is why they recruit creatively. Chris will accompany you through these pages and will cover many topics and points as you embark on a journey towards a fulfilling and successful career.

Although there are many textbooks on how to find a job in Canada, none offer a complete guide and companion throughout the entire journey whether you are a Canadian citizen, new Canadian or work permit–holder. This book will get you thinking about how you can establish a career path and/or transition to a new one.

To say the least, navigating the challenges and changes presented by Canada's market and economy has been difficult; however, finding the best career opportunity is unlikely to abate.

As more and more people make the decision to control their own career choices, the need for career hunting tools becomes greater. The intent of this book is to provide a helpful guide and explanatory information to job seekers of all sorts. If you are one of these job seekers, may this book help you find the career you have been searching for! Good luck!"
Tamer Hegazy, Auditor, Management Accountant and Training Specialist

"Marc is genuinely a gem in the HR world. Marc is always cheerful, helpful, and so creative it hurts and a professional making a huge difference in hundreds and hundreds of people's lives every single day! It is a privilege to know Marc and to collaborate with him, provide TorontoJobs.ca articles for their newsletters and to volunteer as a resume critique and speaker at his job fairs!"
Colleen Clarke, Career Specialist and Corporate Trainer

TALES FROM THE RECRUITER

A Canadian Recruiter's Perspective on How to Get That Perfect Job

MARC BELAICHE, CPA, CA
President, TorontoJobs.ca

Editor: Shannon Brisco

Marquis Book Printing
Quebec, Canada, 2013

Tales from the Recruiter™

A Canadian Recruiter's Perspective on How to Get That Perfect Job

ISBN 978-0-9919380-0-1

Distributed by:
TorontoJobs.ca Publications Inc.
160 Traders Boulevard East, Ste. 101
Mississauga, Ontario
L4Z 3K7
905-566-5627 (phone); 905-566-1179 (fax)
info@TorontoJobs.ca
www.TorontoJobs.ca

Edited by: Shannon Briso
Design and Layout: Jill Walker
Printed and Bound in Canada
Marquis Book Printing

Tales from the Recruiter
Table of Contents

PREFACE

When I was growing up I dreamed of becoming a rock star, professional athlete, policeman, fireman, or even a superhero. Little did I know I would end up being a recruiter!

Initially, I had no idea what recruiting (or "head-hunting" as some people refer to it) was, other than interviewing people and getting them jobs. Throughout my career I've realized that there are significant implications in this work – helping companies find the *right* person, guiding people in their careers, giving advice to job seekers, negotiating job offers, understanding the job market... the list goes on and on. Additionally, I know that there is so much a job seeker needs to be aware of throughout a job search. This book provides insider secrets to land your dream job and move up the corporate ladder.

Regardless of the level of experience over the years – whether a senior executive with many years of know-how or a student looking for their first summer job – everyone has common questions and issues. Some questions include: How is the market? What salary should I be expecting? How should I put together my resume?

I have based this book on those very questions which I hear over and over again when I am speaking at various engagements. Although the passage of time may change the answers to these questions to a certain extent, the substance of the answers generally stays the same.

Recently, being interviewed for a radio segment, the host asked me, "What are the worst things someone can do during an interview?" I answered with some of the more common things like being late for an interview, not speaking clearly and avoiding eye contract with the interviewer. The host noted that those things haven't changed in the past 50 years or more.

While this is true, the fact is we're all in different situations with our own frame of reference. Some of us know these things naturally, some of us need to be reminded, and some of us need to learn these things for the first time.

Given the limited number of people I can personally speak with during the course of a day, I know that there are so many people that I will never have the opportunity to meet in person. This book contains much of my advice that I want to share and I hope that you will be able to use some of the content of this book to help in your job search and/or to rise through your career.

The fact is, although some may call me an expert in recruitment because of my years of experience, I don't know all the answers. I will share with you my personal thoughts and suggestions in this book based on my experience.

For example, when asked to give some input on the format of a resume, I will typically mention something like "If you ask 10 recruiters their suggestions, you'll probably get 10 different answers." Every "expert" will have an opinion on how a resume should be presented. Do you go with the majority? Do you go with the one you trust the most? I always think you should go with what you feel is most comfortable for you and represents you the best. I don't pretend to have all the answers, but I will share ideas with you that you should find useful.

As I was doing research for this book to see what resources are out there for job seekers, I found many books; however, I didn't find one that really encompassed everything recruiters do and their perspective on the job hunting process in a simple and easy-to-read format. I wanted to share a recruiter's perspective that was understandable as much to a senior executive as to a teenager. So, while a lot of people have written books to help people with their careers, I wanted to do something a little more basic and down-to-earth.

This book is written in layman's terms – I have tried to keep the terminology and concepts as simple as possible. In doing so, I asked a broad range of people to review drafts of this book: from my teenage daughter to my mother and from unemployed to happily employed individuals. I asked them to circle in red anything they couldn't understand and made edit changes as a result of the feedback.

While there are no guarantees in life, I can assure you that if you practice the majority of the tips I've suggested, you will be in a stronger position to get the job you want, be more confident in negotiating a job offer and be in a better position to advance your career.

I hope you enjoy this book. I had fun writing it, drawing on a collection of real life situations that I have encountered in the recruitment industry.

ACKNOWLEDGEMENTS

To Ann, my dearest and beautiful wife, my best friend and business partner, who has been so supportive through all our years together. We have made it through a lot of ups and downs over the years in our lives, both personal and professional. I'm grateful to have you as my wife and best friend, and I appreciate your understanding and commitment to the goals that we've set over the years. I love you.

To Mercedes and Milana, who are the most beautiful daughters anyone could wish for and I am extremely proud of them. My love for you both is endless and I thank you for understanding all the long hours that your Mom and Dad have both put into our business.

To my Mom, Dad and two "big brothers" Oscar and Alan who have guided, supported, advised me, and shared their stories over the years – without you, there's no way I'd be where I am now.

To all my clients I have had over the years that I have helped to find new employees: there's nothing truly more satisfying than being a recruiter who presents you with a candidate you hire and who grows with your organization for many years.

To all the job seekers I've had the pleasure of connecting with, advising, working with and placing with my clients. It's been a pleasure working with you throughout the years.

To my current and former associates at TorontoJobs.ca and TorontoEntrepreneurs.ca, who have put in tremendous effort to keep pushing the company forward with every additional project that has been completed, every event that we've put on or attended and every contact that we've made with both job seekers and clients. Without all of you, the company would be nowhere near what it has become.

To Rachel Mitchell, Manager of Business Development at TorontoJobs.ca, who started with the company in 2006 and has led so many initiatives, been the driver of many changes and improvements within the organization and has been rock solid all these years. Many ideas that Rachel has generated over the years have led to charting the direction of the company – we wouldn't be where we are now if it weren't for you Rachel.

Tales from the Recruiter

To Jill Walker, who designed this book and did all the layout for it – thank you for your great ideas.

To the many coaches, resume writers and career consultants who have allowed me to speak with them about tactics, trends and issues facing job seekers: thank you.

To all my friends, business colleagues and former co-workers who have given advice, suggestions and referrals of all kinds over the years: there are so many of you to thank. I wouldn't be able to thank everyone here, but I wanted to highlight Andre Cohen, Peter Steger, Bernie Mandl, John-Paul Strasler, Earl Altman, Joe Marchello, Pierre Janelle, David Wojcik, Jim Gerraghty, Laurel Stultz, Laurel Ancheta, Dan Casey, Richard Leblanc and Jean Wong.

To the many contacts from schools, employment centres, associations and other networking groups who have allowed me to present to their students and clients on job search techniques and have been big supporters of TorontoJobs.ca and our career fairs.

To the many media outlets who have given me the honour of appearing on their television and radio shows on topics as diverse as what to wear to interviews, to what not to do at company holiday parties.

To the Canadian Institute of Chartered Accountants (CICA), Institute of Chartered Accountants of Ontario (ICAO) and Chartered Professional Accountants of Canada (CPA Canada) for allowing me to present at many of their events, and for providing me with the CPA and CA designations that I've been able to use to gain instant credibility with clients, job seekers and other business leaders in order to progress in my professional career.

To all my fellow members in the Human Resources Professionals Association (HRPA) who I've worked with, volunteered together at many HRPA events and networked with, including Angie Bjornson, Cindy Size and Doris Steimle.

To my friend Sandy Thomson, a recruiting industry veteran with whom I've shared many unique stories about the industry. There's never a dull day in this business.

To the many people who have read the drafts of this book and have given me tremendous feedback. These include Alan Wargo, Joseph Thomas and Steven Isidori to name just a few. Thank you for all your time and energy that you've put into reading the drafts as well as your excellent feedback and genuine honesty.

To Shannon Brisco, Editor of this book, who spent countless hours on the various drafts and discussing the major and minor parts of the manuscript – thank you for being patient with me!

Thanks to all of you for making my career in the recruiting industry more interesting and enjoyable!

CHAPTER ONE
CHRIS THE RECRUITER

Chris is now 46 years old. After 15 years of marriage and two children, he has learned how to balance work and family responsibilities.

He completed his university business degree when he was 22. Afterwards, he worked for an accounting firm performing audits of companies for a few years, but never really enjoyed the work. He continued in accounting roles for a few more years with an insurance company but never felt it was his calling.

Chris enjoyed working with people but his accounting work didn't give him an opportunity to utilize his interpersonal skills. He was frustrated. When he was 29, he didn't know what to do in his career. He was making good money in accounting, but he wasn't happy with his job.

He started applying every so often to some job openings for accountants, but really didn't see anything in any job description that appealed to him. He applied for some sales positions because he had heard that you needed to be extroverted to do sales; however, he couldn't envision doing door-to-door sales and those were the opportunities that kept coming up. He didn't know what he was going to do or where he was going to go.

One Saturday morning he noticed an ad for a "Recruiter/Sales Representative." The ad said the company was looking for someone with a business degree who was outgoing, liked working with people and was interested in sales. The company advertising the position was a recruiting firm.

He didn't know what a recruiter did or how recruiting firms worked. He remembered someone calling him years earlier from a recruiting firm, but he didn't remember much of the conversation and never heard back from them. He applied for the recruiter position anyway since the description seemed appealing.

A couple of days later he received a call from the recruiting firm that he applied to. The woman, Sandy, was friendly on the phone and asked him to come in for an interview to talk about the position further. He really didn't know what to ask her about the position because he wasn't aware of what was involved in the role, but he agreed to the interview.

Sandy started the interview by introducing herself as the director of staffing at the recruiting firm. She was responsible both for finding people for the firm as well as helping her clients find staff.

She asked him about his work experience, salary expectations, what he was looking to do in his career, where he wanted to be in five years, etc. Although he was comfortable answering questions about what he had done, he didn't really know what to say about the future. As much as he wanted to get out of accounting, he didn't know what he really wanted; this interview was also a bit of self-reflection for him.

Sandy made him feel comfortable and probed Chris with additional questions about what he liked to do, his strengths, what motivated him, etc. He knew that he liked talking to people, but didn't know how that could be turned into an actual job or career. He told her that he didn't really like accounting that much, but that his family had pushed him to get into it because it was a "good career". He actually wanted to be a disc jockey on the radio when he was growing up!

Sandy said that Chris might be interested in exploring becoming a recruiter. He asked for additional information about what the role entailed, what he would be doing and most importantly, how he would get paid.

She started by explaining that people typically don't grow up thinking they're going to be a recruiter and most usually fall into the industry by chance, sometimes by meeting a recruiter in the industry accidentally. For example, Sandy herself had met a recruiter by chance and after doing some research herself, decided to get into the industry and had been in it for 10 years already. Sandy said that most people have high aspirations for their careers when they're younger, such as being at a "sea level" position.

Chris was too afraid to ask what a "sea level" position was during the interview because he didn't want to appear ignorant. He thought it must have something to do with where a company was located – "The closer to the ocean, the better…" he guessed.

He later found out that "sea level" was actually "C-level" and referred to positions such as Chief Financial Officer (CFO), Chief Executive Officer (CEO), Chief Information Officer (CIO), etc. The "sea" was actually the letter "C" representing the word "chief". Was he ever glad he didn't ask Sandy what she meant!

Sandy continued to explain that recruiting is a career that can be both very lucrative and rewarding. The industry literally employed hundreds of thousands of people around the world. She explained it's not for people who are shy but rather for those who are very driven and see the glass as half-full. She said that it requires someone very motivated who liked networking.

Chris, at the time, thought networking had to do with computers and heard that some people had jobs networking computers. He didn't think he was an IT guy and wondered why Sandy thought that he might like networking.

She explained, very basically, that a recruiter's role is to find companies looking for people to hire, to look for people searching for positions and put the right ones together. She described it as being similar to a real estate agent who looks for a buyer and a seller for a house.

Sandy continued by saying that recruiters use whatever methods they could to find both job seekers and clients.

There were a number of ways a recruiter would find job seekers, she explained. For example:

- They could advertise open job positions and review resumes from people who applied to the position;
- They could reach out to business contacts, previous classmates, friends, family and relatives and ask for referrals to anyone they knew looking for a job; and/or
- They could look through resume databases of job seekers who posted their resumes online.

There were also a number of ways a recruiter could find organizations looking to hire, or clients, such as:

- Again, asking for referrals from business contacts, previous classmates, friends, family and relatives;
- Reaching out to companies who had advertised job openings and asking if they needed assistance in finding a candidate; and/or
- Going to breakfasts, lunches or dinners where hiring people, such as human resources, or HR, professionals, might attend.

Tales from the Recruiter

Sandy explained that recruiting was about finding appropriate people for organizations looking to hire and that recruiters got paid by the organizations who hired those candidates. As a result, a recruiter would make money earning commission (or a percentage) of what the organization paid the recruiting firm.

Chris still didn't really understand how it worked, but he made a lot of notes in the meeting so he could ask his family and friends.

After their meeting, Sandy suggested that Chris think about their conversation and reach out to her if he was interested in discussing it further.

Chris spoke with a number of people after the meeting with Sandy. He asked his family and friends about their thoughts of him becoming a recruiter and if they knew anyone or anything about the industry. He called a few recruiters that were referred to him to ask their thoughts and was met with a mix of both favourable and unfavourable feedback about the industry. Some recruiters didn't even call him back. This left Chris with a negative opinion about the industry from the outset. Chris thought that if he got into the recruiting industry he would try to improve its image by making a commitment to return all calls.

Notwithstanding some of the negative feedback he heard about the business, he became very interested in the industry and continued researching.

After meeting Sandy two more times and asking as many questions as he could think of, he was ready to make the leap into recruiting. At the time, he was single, had no mortgage and thought that if it didn't work out, he could just find a position for himself! He was willing to give it a go. That was 17 years ago.

In his first 10 years as a recruiter, Chris learned as much as possible about the recruiting industry. He worked for a large, multinational recruiting firm for six years as well as a small local firm for four years. Seven years ago, Chris decided to start up his own recruiting firm and has been growing his business ever since. He works with other recruiters in his company helping people find jobs and connects with companies to find the right people for their organizations. His wife also works part-time in the business with Chris.

CHAPTER TWO

THE HOLIDAY PARTY

It was an unexpected encounter at a somewhat crowded house party on a Saturday night. Chris was there with his wife.

Being an extroverted guy, Chris attended as many events as he could. He did this not only because he liked people, but also because he enjoyed helping people in their careers and knew that every time he went to any kind of dinner, networking or social event, he would eventually meet someone who was looking for a job. This party was going to be no different.

Once people found out what Chris did for a living, conversations would almost inevitably turn into discussions about the job market and searching for a job. Recruiters always seem to find people to talk to who are looking for a job or a new career or know someone who is.

Ann was making small talk with another person at the party, but what was really on her mind was her job. She was unhappy in her job. Extremely unhappy. She no longer liked the company she was working for. She didn't like her boss. She didn't like the people she worked with. She was feeling the stress of having too much work, not being recognized for her hard work and just needed a change.

Typically, when Ann left work on Friday nights she already dreaded the thought of returning Monday morning. Sunday nights she would usually have a pain in her stomach thinking about going into work the next morning. This night was no different. She was chatting with someone at the party, but wasn't really hearing what the other person was saying. She was preoccupied and had been unhappy for months, but she didn't know how to go about finding a new job.

Ann's friend Carlos had invited her to come with him to the party. Ann had confided in him many times over the last year about her job and how it was draining her, mentally and physically. In fact, before they arrived at the party, Ann had spent 20 minutes in the car complaining to Carlos about how her co-worker had just been given a promotion ahead of Ann, even though he had been at the company less time than Ann. The co-worker wasn't even doing a great job, according to Ann. The co-worker did, however, know how to "play the game" and went to lunch with the president of the company at least once a week and constantly talked with other co-workers about football.

Carlos himself actually enjoyed his job, but always had his ear to the ground to hear about that next "big opportunity" that might be just around the corner. He had moved to the city from a small town when he was young and his career had taken flight. He always seemed to be in the right place at the right time and seemed to come across job opportunities easily.

At the party, Carlos was chatting with a well-dressed gentleman he had just met, named Rajesh. Rajesh had been invited to the party by the host after they had met at a recent networking event. Other than the host, Rajesh didn't know a single person at the party until he met Carlos. Rajesh didn't know many people in the city either, except for his wife who had stayed at home to be with their kids, and a few other New Canadians he had met through job searching. Rajesh and his family had recently immigrated from abroad and they were trying to get to know the people and learn the local customs. He was happy to be able to meet people that would be able to help him figure out how to make a better life. He was thrilled to have been invited to the party.

At that moment, Ann finished her conversation with another person and turned to the bar to refresh her glass of wine and accidently bumped into Chris. They both apologized at the same time.

Smiling at each other, they exchanged introductions and talked about how they knew the host. Sure enough, shortly after starting their conversation, the subject of work came up and they asked each other what they did for a living.

As soon as Ann learned that Chris was a recruiter, a slight smile came upon her face. Coming to the party may now possibly have been worthwhile. Ann didn't really know what a recruiter did, but thought that Chris could be the key to her getting another job. Little did she know just how helpful Chris was going to be over the coming weeks.

Ann was cautious about explaining to Chris how much she hated her job because she didn't know him. She was always a little paranoid about talking about job issues as she didn't want it getting back to her boss. She was, however, curious to know what Chris did and how he might be able to help her.

Ann quietly asked Chris, "How's the job market these days?"

Chris replied, "It's actually not too bad. There are always certain pockets of the market that do well and others that are slow. There's a real cycle in the job market with supply and demand that are never in perfect harmony. There are constantly changing hot and cold areas and they seem to change fairly regularly. For example, for a period of time there's a high demand for informational technology, or IT people. Then a few years later IT is in low demand and accountants are in high demand. And then accountants are in low demand and sales people become in high demand, etc. Being a recruiter, I tend to get jobs to fill from my clients from those areas that are hotter at a particular time, but there are always companies looking for staff."

Ann asked, "What's hot right now?"

Chris had learned over the years that he didn't want to say anything that might discourage a job seeker. The reality is that there are always people who find jobs in every area, regardless of experience or skills. Although he didn't really know who Ann was or if she was even looking for a job, he was always on the lookout to meet good candidates so that he could try placing them with his clients. Chris didn't want to come across as too pushy either, as he genuinely liked helping people find their new jobs or careers. He knew over the years that he preferred to tailor an answer to the specific person rather than provide a general overview of the market.

Being a recruiter, Chris typically liked to be the one asking the questions. He always remembered the saying "You have two ears and only one mouth. So, you should listen twice as much as you talk!"

In Chris' experience he might ultimately be able to get Ann to come in for an interview in his office and perhaps place her with one of his clients. From what he could quickly gather, having met with and interviewed thousands of people in his career, Ann was presentable, friendly and had excellent communication skills. These are some of the elements that Chris knew his clients like right from the start, aside from a person's experience.

Instead of responding directly to her question, he asked Ann, "Are you looking for a job?"

Ann whispered so that others around her wouldn't hear her, "Well, I have been thinking about possibly finding something different."

Chris asked her in a quiet voice what she was looking for, knowing that she was trying to be discreet.

"I'm looking for something in the accounting area." Ann began to get a comfortable feel that she might be able to speak to Chris on a confidential basis. "I'm looking for a senior accountant type of role... something where I can really be of value to an organization and somewhere I would be appreciated."

Chris got the message. He had met many people looking for jobs over the years. Chris was already picking up the message that Ann was unhappy in her job and that she might be looking for something else by her words.

"Have you been looking for a new job for a long time?" asked Chris. From the answer to this question, he would be able to determine a lot. If she had been looking for a new position for a long time and had been on many interviews, it could mean that Ann might not be too marketable from a recruiter's perspective. If Ann answered that she'd been looking for a while but hadn't interviewed with anyone, it could mean that her resume didn't stand out or her skills were not in high demand. If Ann answered that she was just starting to look, she might not have her resume ready.

Ultimately, from Chris' perspective, if she wasn't that active or hadn't been looking for a long time, he'd be in a better position to get the first chance at finding her a new job, before his competitors in other recruiting firms could try. So a lot was riding on the answer to this one question.

Ann replied, "Well, I've had my eyes open for anything that might come up for a few months now, but I haven't done anything as of yet. I haven't even updated my resume. I'm so busy both at work and in my personal life that I really haven't had a moment to do anything. The last time I went on a real interview was probably 10 years ago. At my current job I didn't even have to do a resume because I got the position through a referral from someone I knew and they never even asked me for a resume. When they hired me it wasn't really an interview – it was basically just an informal meeting and I got the job after meeting my boss once. We hit it off instantly – he liked me and I liked what I heard."

Chris suggested to Ann, "I can certainly help you find a job if you want me to. I can suggest some ideas for your resume and can give you tips on how to find a job also. I've been in recruiting for a while now, so I can help you with your search."

Ann replied, "That would be great. Do I have to pay anything for you to help me?"

Chris answered, "No. First of all, I like to help people in their job search – that's what I love to do. I do this for a living. My goal, ultimately, is to help you find a job. If I'm able to place you in a job with one of my clients, I would get paid by my client. If you find a position on your own, you wouldn't owe me anything either. My hope either way would be that you might remember me when you're in your new company. Perhaps you will let me know of any positions your company is looking to fill when they're hiring someone. Secondly, you don't, and should never, have to pay a recruiter to help you find a job. Recruiters get paid by their clients, not by job seekers. We're not career coaches either. Coaches do get paid by the person looking for a job, but that's the way they make their living. Although they would want to help you find a position, coaches don't typically get paid extra for finding you a position. Since recruiters get paid by their clients, they are generally happy to meet with people looking for a job - it means they can build their database of candidates who they might be able to place today or in the future with their clients."

Ann asked, "Oh, okay. I didn't know recruiters didn't charge. How do I sign up?"

Chris answered, "You don't need to 'sign up'. Let's just set up a time to meet in my office and we can talk about what you're looking for and how I can help you."

"That would be great!" smiled Ann.

While speaking with Rajesh, Carlos overheard Ann's exclamation and turned his head to find out what she was excited about.

Ann said to Carlos, "I just met Chris. Chris is a recruiter. He's offered to help me find a job. We were just talking about setting up a time to meet in his office to talk about my job search."

Carlos said, "Nice to meet you Chris, and that's great if you can help Ann find something. I know recruiters can be very helpful in finding people jobs. A recruiter actually placed me in my current position a few years ago. Do you work for a large recruiting firm?"

"Actually, I own a recruiting firm that I started up a number of years ago," said Chris.

"Interesting!" smiled Carlos.

Rajesh, who was still standing close to Carlos, politely asked if he could also meet with Chris because he was also looking for a position. Chris smiled and said "Of course you can."

Rajesh asked, "Is there a cost?"

Ann and Chris looked at each other and smiled.

Chris answered, "No, there's no cost involved. I'm happy to meet with all three of you if you'd like."

Carlos, Ann and Rajesh all looked at each other and nodded their heads. After all, it's not every day that you meet a recruiter on a casual basis.

Even though he wasn't actively searching for a position, Carlos thought to himself that it wouldn't hurt for him to also meet with a recruiter. He also had wondered how the recruiting industry worked and what recruiters actually did every day.

The four agreed to meet at Chris' office the following Wednesday at 5:30 p.m. Chris asked them to bring whatever questions they had about finding a job as well as their resumes if they had them available.

It was getting late and the party was finishing up. Chris gave his three new connections his business card with his address and phone number. Ann, Carlos and Rajesh all lived near to Chris' office so it would be convenient for them to meet there.

On the way home, Chris told his wife about meeting Ann, Carlos and Rajesh and that he was going to help them with their job searches. He knew that he was going to have three new candidates that he could possibly place with his clients, either now or in the future.

As Carlos and Ann were driving home, Ann was excited about having made the connection with Chris. Her attitude was completely different than it had been earlier upon arriving at the party. She talked to Carlos all the way home about how motivated she was in finding a new job and how she thought Chris was going to be able to help her find something.

Although Carlos didn't get a chance to speak in the car because of Ann's constant excited chatter on their way home, he himself was also looking forward to meeting Chris. Carlos thought that Chris might be able to help him reach his career aspirations, give him some advice and perhaps even answer some questions about a hidden passion that he had – starting up his own business.

Rajesh was thrilled to have met both Carlos and Chris as he was in the process of building his contacts. He started the night not knowing anyone other than the host of the party. He left knowing that the meeting Wednesday could be the start of something good for him. He had some optimism about finding a job in Canada. He couldn't wait to get home to let his wife know about the chance meeting.

CHAPTER THREE
THE "STUDENTS"

ANN

When Ann was young she dreamed of owning her own flower store. She always thought that was her life's mission. However, as she grew up she realized what was involved in running a business and she knew that unless she won the lottery or received an inheritance, it wasn't going to become a reality.

Being the youngest of four children, she always received guidance from her older siblings about what to do in life. They would tell her "Go to college, get a job at a good company and just stay there." They never told her what kind of job or how to go about it.

She would get job search tips from her college friends, but realized later they really didn't have a clue themselves as to how to find a job. For example, she remembered one of her classmates telling her to print her resume on pink or yellow paper so it would stand out when companies were looking through resumes.

She thought about another friend who told her "Ann, don't ask how much a position is paying in your interview because that's rude. Wait until the person interviewing you asks you what you're looking for… and when they do, tell them you didn't know and that you would take anything reasonable."

Her understanding of how to find a job was limited, but she always seemed to be in the right place at the right time and never had to search hard to find a job. Her parents found her a summer job when she was in college as an accounting clerk for a small manufacturing company.

When she graduated in accounting from college, one of her professors referred her to an opportunity with a local retailer who was looking for a bookkeeper. She didn't really have a lot of experience for the role, but she got the job and gained a lot of experience in accounting in the next two years.

Ann got her current position through a contact she had from school. Her friend was leaving the job to stay home with her kids and had referred Ann to the controller of the company as a possible replacement. Ann met the controller and got the job on the spot. She didn't even have to write a resume because the controller needed someone immediately. Ann has been at the same company, a medium-sized distribution company, for four years as a general accountant.

She's currently unhappy in her role and needs a change. Her boss has put a lot of pressure on her and doesn't respect the quality of her work. He is always asking for her to stay late and Ann isn't getting recognized for the hard work she does.

What has made it even worse is that Ann feels she is underpaid for her work. Since Ann handles the company's payroll, she knows that someone new at her company who has a lot less work experience than her is getting paid more than her.

Everything just seems to be crumbling for Ann at this time. Nothing seems to be going right for her. She needs a new position as soon as possible.

Now 28, Ann is single and has never been married. She shares a condo with a roommate. She is a little shy and isn't career-oriented, yet knows that she is unhappy with her current job. She had been introduced to Carlos through a mutual friend six months earlier and their friendship blossomed.

With little experience in job searching, she needs help. She is looking forward to meeting Chris on Wednesday so that she will be able to understand the best way to find another position. She doesn't know where or what to do in her search. She doesn't know where to start with her resume, how to interview, etc. Although she has been working for several years, her job search experience is extremely limited.

CARLOS

Carlos was born in Spain and moved to Canada when he was very young.

Growing up, Carlos had always thought he would be in a position where he would be in charge. He didn't know what that would be, but he always seemed to be in leadership roles. As he progressed through school, he was always team captain of his school football and soccer teams, and was also the debating champion in university.

Carlos was constantly the one motivating others. He was continuously leading. Carlos always understood the big picture of life and was ahead of his peers. This served him well in both his work and professional life.

When he graduated with a computer science degree from university, he had scored high marks and was in demand by employers. He was immediately hired by a large bank in a role that paid very well for new graduates. The bank had actually gone on-campus to recruit new students just like Carlos.

As Carlos gained more experience in his professional career, he showed great leadership in his roles and was promoted very quickly. He moved to other companies when he felt that he had reached his maximum potential with a particular employer. He gained progressive experience in several roles, staying with each company for three to seven years.

He had been the President of the Information Technology (IT) Association in the city - an impressive accomplishment that had launched his career even further and faster as it helped him build his contacts.

He had found his current position through a recruiter who presented him with the opportunity. He beat out four other candidates for the position, and is now the Director of IT at a major insurance company. He is well paid and oversees a department of 35 people, with six people reporting directly to him.

Although he is happy in his current role, he likes to be in control of his career. He always seems to want the next best job as he feels that he's always missing out on a better opportunity elsewhere. However, he also feels that he may have hit the ceiling when it comes to his career and thinks there is no further room for him to move up in the IT world.

Now 51 years old, Carlos recently divorced his wife after having been married 22 years. He has two sons in college. He works and plays hard. He plays soccer two nights a week, has a lot of friends and attends many social events, networking opportunities and dinners.

Carlos was looking forward to meeting Chris on Wednesday to find out what opportunities were out there, what the status of the job market was and how to go about possibly starting up a business. He was curious to hear from Chris on any tips he had to help Carlos with his career, networking to find a job, and anything else that he could find out to be able to advance his career. Carlos was also curious about how Chris started up his business and the challenges that he faced.

<u>RAJESH</u>

Rajesh grew up in a large family in India. He was the oldest of five children. He was taught by his mother and father that "family always comes first".

When he married fifteen years ago, following the same traditions as he was raised, Rajesh and his wife agreed to maintain the family as their priority. They now have two daughters aged four and eight.

As he progressed through school in India, he always received high marks in his courses. He graduated with a mechanical engineering degree.

He was promoted through various large organizations into technical engineering and project manager positions. Eventually, he became the general manager of a large organization in India. The pay was good and he had a good life. He was well-respected and lived in a nice home.

He had heard of others moving from India to other countries with the promise of a better life and living standards. He had been told that Canada could provide a well-paying job and that jobs were plenty. He made the decision to move to give his daughters a greater opportunity.

He went through the entire immigration process that took many months. He was told that those who "win" the right to immigrate to Canada are determined based on a point scoring system. The more points the better the chances of being accepted to Canada. Among other reasons, he was given more points because he was an engineer. He was ultimately accepted into Canada and relocated with his wife and two children. He made the move six months ago.

Upon arrival, he quickly started looking for a new job with the expectation that he would find something before long. Unfortunately, he's realized over the last few months that his experience abroad didn't matter very much in Canada. He has sent out hundreds of resumes since he arrived, but has received a handful of rejection letters. He has never been called in for an interview by a company. He has heard through other New Canadians that his foreign experience wasn't valued in Canada and didn't understand why. Other Newcomers also had excellent foreign experience but that wasn't recognized either. The other New Canadians that had landed before him took jobs that were well below their area of expertise just to make ends meet. Many had started to run out of their savings. They accepted lower paying jobs just to make money, such as driving taxi cabs, working in construction, or whatever other jobs they could find. They were being taken advantage of by employers who were preying on their desperation.

Rajesh was getting nervous. Rajesh and his wife had begun having difficulties in their relationship as a result of discovering the challenges of finding a job in Canada. They were starting to spend family savings to pay for food, rent and clothing. They started questioning whether their move was the right decision. What happened to the better life they were expecting? When will this get better? How could this be happening? They were living in an apartment with two kids and couldn't go very much longer spending their savings.

Rajesh was trying very hard to find a job. He didn't want to settle for something like driving a taxi like some of the other stories he had heard, because it wouldn't be relevant to his educational and work experience, but was starting to get nervous that he might need to do that.

He was going to employment centres each day that were funded by the government to learn the best ways of finding a job. He was going to any seminar that he could to learn about how to put his resume together and was learning more as he went along. However, the more he went to these seminars and spent time at the employment centres, the more he felt he wasn't getting ahead, although the people there were very helpful. He was discouraged and was getting very anxious. He felt like a new graduate with no experience. He was really upset.

He was looking forward to meeting Chris on Wednesday to get help with his job search, understand the way job searches really worked in Canada, and ultimately to get a job as soon as possible. He had received some good feedback on how to improve his resume by a few people, but he wanted to understand why he wasn't being contacted for any interviews. He also wanted to learn some ways to network when he had so few contacts.

CHAPTER FOUR

"WHAT DO RECRUITERS ACTUALLY DO?"

The four met for the first time that Wednesday at 5:30 p.m. in Chris' office.

After chatting about the party the previous Saturday, they were all excited about sitting down to talk about recruiters and how Chris could help each of them.

"So, have each of you thought about what you'd like to talk about? Anything specific you'd like to discuss?" asked Chris.

Carlos started by saying, "First of all, I'd like to thank you for staying late today to speak with us." Chris smiled. "I think the one question that I have and I think that Rajesh and Ann, I'm sure, have thought about also is what do recruiters actually do every day?"

Chris responded, "No problem with staying late as I'm happy to help anytime. Recruiters actually do a lot of things. Recruiting is a fairly simple business – they match people with jobs and companies with people. However, there is a lot more to it, as it's both an art and a science."

"From a simple perspective, recruiters focus on finding candidates for jobs and finding companies that are looking to hire for their open positions and matching the two together. There really is a lot of work involved in doing the matching part. People think that it's easy to find candidates and clients, but it really takes a lot of time for both. I compare it to finding a house – it's hard to find a perfect house, right?"

Rajesh, Carlos and Ann all nodded.

"Well, I think of recruiting as helping someone find their perfect job and helping a company find their perfect employee," said Chris. "In real estate, it's very difficult to find a perfect house for someone. The people buying the house usually have to sacrifice on something that they want – maybe they're not getting the finished basement they wanted or the size of kitchen that they were hoping to get. Similarly, the people selling their house might have to sell their house at a price lower than what they had expected. Likewise, in recruiting it's difficult to get a perfect job for a candidate and hard for a company to find a perfect candidate for a position. Both sides typically need to sacrifice on something for a recruiter to be able to make a placement. Perhaps the candidate takes a job that is not exactly what they were looking for – for example, the company is further from their home than they expected or is smaller than they are used to. Perhaps a company needs to train that new employee more than they were expecting or might need to pay more than they wanted. If I have a job seeker or a client not wanting to be flexible in what they're willing to accept, there is less of a chance of making a successful placement. It's a recruiter's role to manage each party's expectations to try to make a successful placement."

Ann asked, "Chris, can you give any examples of when you had a candidate that had to be flexible on something?"

"Well," began Chris, "there was a candidate a couple of weeks ago who was working downtown but lived in the suburbs. It was taking her an hour to get to work and another hour to get home. This was happening every day. She was earning $35,000 a year. When I first met her, she told me she was looking to make between $35,000 and $40,000 if she was going to make a move to another position. It turns out I found her a job that she really liked that was down the street from her house, but the company only offered her $32,000 which was $3,000 less than what she was currently earning. At first she thought there was no way that she would take the offer. However, we started talking about her current job and the amount of time it was taking for her to get to her current job each day and each week. We discussed her gas costs of driving to and from the train station. We then calculated the costs of parking at the train station, the cost of her monthly transit pass and the amount of time she was spending either at work or commuting to work. After outlining all the costs and time involved, it turned out that even though this new offer was less overall money than what she was at currently, she was actually going to be making more money - the money she would save by not having to pay her parking and monthly transit pass alone, which was in after-tax dollars, would still give her more income if she took the $32,000 job. She realized that she would be earning more by actually earning less! When she added the fact that she wouldn't be spending so much time travelling to and from work it became obvious to her that it was better for her to be making less money but be closer to home. In this case, the candidate was flexible."

"Interesting story…" said Carlos, "the dollar amount doesn't matter – this could apply to senior or junior people."

"Absolutely!" said Chris. "In fact, all the stories and advice that I might share with you are applicable to any level of person and any type of background. I hear the same types of questions from all types of people. It doesn't matter who it is. When I present to a group of senior executives I give them the same examples as when I do presentations to a college or university class."

"Good to know!" commented Carlos.

"What is a typical day like for you?" asked Ann.

"Well, every recruiter that I've worked with has their own schedule and does different tasks each day, but here are some things that a recruiter might do on any particular day:

- call companies to try and get business by finding positions for which candidates can be recruited;
- network with candidates and/or clients to find other candidates and/or clients
- interview candidates;
- perform reference checks on a job seeker who a client is looking to hire;
- post open positions online;
- prepare people for interviews that they are going on with recruiter's clients;
- meet with clients to go over their staffing needs; and/or
- attend networking events.

As you can see, there's a lot of variety within the job," remarked Chris.

"Sounds like an interesting job!" said Carlos.

"I really enjoy what I do!" remarked Chris. "A lot of the people that I've met over the years who have become recruiters don't really know if they're going to like it or not. Some don't like it. Some stay in it for a while and then get out. There have been some recruiters I've worked with who I thought would be successful but they just can't do it. Others I wondered how they could possibly do well in the industry and then they are phenomenal. You could have someone who has all kinds of degrees and designations and an excellent education but just can't make it in the industry. Then you could have a high school drop-out who just instinctively understands the business, knows how to make a 'deal' happen and is extremely successful in recruiting. Some people in the industry look at recruiting as a job while others look at it as a career. I personally think it's a career choice. Either way, it's a fun industry, but there is definitely an element of sales in the role. You have to sometimes sell a candidate on a job and sometimes you have to sell a candidate to a client. I personally like the placements where everything fits into place and I don't have to sell anything. However, recruiters earn commission based on the business they do so they need to sell. I like to think of recruiting as advising or consulting rather than selling."

"I hope you don't mind me asking this, but how do recruiters get paid?" asked Ann.

"Typically, recruiters who work in recruiting firms get paid either a base salary plus commission or they earn 100% straight commission," explained Chris. "The amount of their base salary depends on their experience; the commission that they earn depends on the placements, or revenues, that they generate. If they're on straight commission, they get a high rate of commission because they're not earning a base salary and are taking all the risk. Some recruiters, in a good market, can make $500,000 a year or more, but those are people that have been in the business for a long time and have a good base of clients."

Everyone's eyes lit up. "Wow!" said Ann. "I had no idea."

"I think I'm in the wrong line of work…" chuckled Carlos.

"It takes time to get there – years, not months. It's also a very cyclical business, so in a bad economic market recruiters don't do very well. Commission really depends on how the job market is. I also want to note that I'm referring to a recruiter who works in an employment agency, finding employees for their clients. There are also 'corporate recruiters' which is something different. That type of recruiter works for a company and finds employees for their own company. Corporate recruiters typically make a fixed salary and generally don't earn commission for finding people. Although, sometimes they might get a small added bonus depending on how many people they find for their organizations. These corporate recruiters usually work hard and they attend job fairs, interview a lot of job seekers, etc. Recruiting, especially in a staffing firm, is a great career choice, but not many people even get to the first stage of finding out what it's all about."

"Since we're at it, I've always wanted to ask, but was afraid to – what is the difference between a recruiting firm and a staffing agency?" asked Ann.

Chris smiled, "Feel free to ask anything – that's why we're here! You'll hear all kinds of terms like staffing agencies, recruiting firms, employment agencies, head-hunters, executive search firms, staffing companies, etc. They are all basically the same, just with different names. They have companies, or 'clients', that pay them to find employees for their companies. The recruiting firms, or staffing agencies, or whatever you want to call them, get paid to find people for their clients. Some recruiting firms like to make up fancy names for what they do, like 'executive recruiters', so that they have the appearance of being different from other recruiting firms, but in essence they do the same thing – finding clients, finding candidates, and matching the two. How they do their work and the types of position they recruit for might vary from firm to firm, but the business is very similar."

Rajesh asked, "How do you usually refer to your company?"

"I usually say 'staffing firm' or 'recruiting firm' but it sometimes depends to whom I'm speaking with," responded Chris. "Sometimes I call myself a 'head-hunter' because some people seem to understand that better."

"Head-hunter sounds so barbaric!" commented Ann.

Chris said, "Yes, I know. I don't really know where that term came from to describe recruiters, but I suppose it's a visual of chopping off heads and serving them on platters for our clients! In baseball, pitchers who throw pitches at the heads of batters are also referred to as head-hunters. I'm always amused when someone calls me a head-hunter. Usually someone calls me that, but then stops themselves and apologizes because they realize they might be offending me. But for me, it's actually quite funny. What other questions do you have? This is fun!"

"What makes a good recruiter?" asked Rajesh.

"Good question, Rajesh!" said Chris. "Recruiters need to have a lot of skills, but generally good recruiters that I've worked with are sympathetic to both client and candidate needs, so they listen well, they ask questions, they uncover issues and are not afraid to address problems early. They're extremely professional and have excellent communication skills. They tend to manage their time very well and they're good with people. They work hard and don't see their job as being 9:00-5:00, Monday to Friday. They will speak with candidates or clients at night or on weekends as well as interview candidates before or after hours if necessary. They will speak at the candidate's or client's level and they never speak down to someone. They treat everyone professionally."

"Thank you Chris," said Rajesh. "By the way, you can all call me Raj. My friends call me Raj."

"Ok," smiled Chris.

"I'm guessing that people ask recruiters a lot of questions?" suggested Ann.

"Yes!" nodded Chris. "I get *a lot* of questions. I get asked about industries, jobs, and about the job market. I'm also asked quite regularly to look at people's resumes and to make suggestions for improvement. People also ask me for advice about job offers they've received and about negotiating terms of a job offer. I believe someone receiving a job offer should always speak with a recruiter about their thoughts around the offer and the role and not just rely on advice from family and friends. Of course it would be a confidential conversation and someone doesn't need to tell the recruiter what company has made the offer. I'm always being asked to give my opinions on people's jobs, their bosses, situations that come up, whether they should accept a job offer, if I know anything about a certain company, etc. I think people might be surprised as to how much recruiters know about companies, what people earn and what goes in the work force."

"What about helping people with their resumes?" asked Raj.

"I will do that for some people," said Chris, "but I'm not a resume writer. There are people that specialize in writing resumes. Recruiters typically don't write resumes, but they will give people feedback when asked. Remember that recruiters aren't paid to help people with their resumes – they are paid for finding people for companies and are paid by those companies. However, in order to do that, a recruiter might need to make a resume look more appealing to a company so that the recruiter's client is more interested in that candidate."

"I've heard recruiting firms work 'contingency', but not sure what that means," said Carlos. "Can you please describe what that means?"

"Most recruiting firms work on a contingency basis," explained Chris, "which means that the recruiter only charges their clients when the client hires one of the candidates that the recruiting firm has presented to them. As such, recruiters want the placement to happen just as much as a candidate who has been interviewed by the client. It can be disappointing at the end of a long search that a client hires a candidate that they found on their own. The recruiter may have spent countless hours finding and interviewing candidates, setting up interviews with candidates for the client over a period of weeks or months and spending a lot of time debriefing with the client and candidates, only to find out that the client ends up hiring another candidate at the last minute."

"Is there anything that recruiters can do to avoid this?" asked Carlos.

"Sadly, no," frowned Chris. "There are other types of recruiting firms that work 'on retainer'. A retainer is an amount a company pays the recruiting firm through the search. For example, a company might pay one-third of the total expected fee when the recruiting firm starts the search, one-third after the first round of interviews and the balance once the successful candidate has accepted the position. So, in the case of a client interviewing candidates from the recruiting firm but not hiring someone at the very end, the recruiting firm would still get two-thirds of the fee. These are usually for executive positions or more specialized searches."

"What about paying a recruiting firm to help us find a job?" asked Raj. "A friend of mine went to a company and they wanted him to pay a few thousand dollars and said they would guarantee him interviews and a job."

"I strongly recommend not paying a company to find you a job," explained Chris. "You should be careful if anyone, not just recruiters, tells you that they can guarantee you a job, or interviews for that matter, especially if they ask you to pay a fee to do that. Recruiting firms get paid by the company, not by the job seeker. It's one thing to pay a resume writer to help you prepare your resume, but quite another thing if someone promises or guarantees that they'll be able to arrange interview with companies for you. No one can guarantee someone a job or interviews, no matter what they might claim," said Chris.

Tales from the Recruiter

"My friend didn't end up doing it because it was a lot of money and didn't really make sense to him," remarked Raj.

"How much do recruiting firms charge their clients?" asked Raj.

"Well, for a full-time position, the fee typically ranges anywhere from 15% to 25% of the first year salary of the candidate. So, for example, a $50,000 placement might result in a $10,000 placement when it's a 20% fee," answered Chris.

"That sounds like a lot of money!" remarked Ann.

"It is, but when you think of all the work involved in finding someone, I think it's fair value," said Chris. "If a company were to do the recruiting themselves their cost would be fairly significant – their employees' time, the cost of an ad, the time going through resumes, etc. In addition, if a company did it themselves they would only be seeing active job seekers (candidates who are actively looking for a new position and applying) rather than passive job seekers (those candidates who are not actively searching for a new position and are not responding to job postings, but may be open to hearing about opportunities if approached). The passive job seekers are harder to find and since recruiting firms are always interviewing people, recruiters have access to those candidates. Recruiting firms have the cost of advertising, salaries, commission, rent and overhead costs, insurance, mileage and parking costs, training costs, etc. People think the fee goes directly to the bottom line of a recruiting firm when they make a placement but there are a lot of costs that go into running a recruiting business. There is also the risk that the client never pays the invoice on a placement, which sometimes happens, and then the recruiting firm needs to send the account to collections or even take legal action against the company, which may result in legal fees."

"I didn't think about all those costs…," said Carlos. "What if you place a person and they don't work out in the position and the company terminates the person or if the person quits? Is there some kind of guarantee on that placement or anything like that?"

Chris replied, "Yes, so while I said before that recruiters can't guarantee anyone a job, they do guarantee their placements with their clients. Typically, on full-time placements that recruiters would make there is anywhere from a three-month to six-month guarantee depending on the level of the person that was placed – the more senior the candidate, the longer the guarantee period. What this means is that if the candidate who has been placed by the recruiting firm with a client leaves the position for whatever reason during the first three to six months of their employment – termination, poor performance, quits, etc. – the recruiting firm will find a replacement for that candidate at no additional cost to the client. There are usually some exceptions to that guarantee, such as if there's a restructuring in the company and the position is being eliminated through no fault of the candidate or if the client doesn't pay the recruiting firm's invoice within a certain period of time."

"What about temporary positions? How do recruiters get paid for those placements?" asked Ann. "I've heard people say that the agency takes a percentage of a person's salary when they're working through an agency on a temporary position."

Chris responded, "On temporary placements recruiters make money on the difference between what they charge the client for each hour that the temporary employee works and what they pay the candidate each hour. For example, the staffing firm may pay someone $20 per hour but charge their client $30 per hour. That works out to a 50% markup – that is, $30 minus $20 equals $10, divided by $20. Staffing firms will try to get as high a markup as possible, sometimes even up to 100%, for examples when they pay the person $50 per hour and charge their client $100 an hour."

"That's unfair…" said Ann.

"It is a business, just like any other," said Chris. "Again, keep in mind that the staffing company has costs also. In the case of a temporary placement, the person is actually the employee of the staffing company, not the client's employee. As such, the staffing company is responsible for paying all of the employee's payroll taxes and vacation pay, called "burdens" in the staffing industry. In addition, the recruiting firm is also paying the employee each week before getting paid by their client, which sometimes takes 30 days or longer to get paid. As such, there are costs to finance that person working. There's also the other costs I mentioned already – advertising, rent, salaries, etc. – which the recruiting firm has to pay. Finally, there's always the risk that the staffing firm doesn't get paid by the company, which means that the staffing company is out the entire amount that they paid to the employee. So, you can see there are costs that the staffing firm does have to pay."

"Ok, I didn't think of it that way," said Ann. "What about guarantees on temporary placements? Do the recruiting firms guarantee those placements too?"

Chris replied, "There are no guarantees on temporary placements since the company pays only for each hour that the person works. If the company needed to terminate a temporary employee because of poor performance, for example, there would be no additional charges since the recruiting firm only charged the company based on the hours worked by the temporary employee each week. On a temporary position the employee does not have a full-time permanent position and is working day-to-day, so typically the person can be let go without the employment agency needing to guarantee anything for their client."

"Makes sense," said Raj.

"What size of companies do you deal with?" Carlos asked.

"I deal with pretty much every size of company… from small to large," said Chris. "I deal with every industry, for example banking, manufacturing, real estate, etc. I also deal with every kind of position – accounting, sales, IT, administrative, etc. Some recruiting firms will specialize in one area or another – perhaps they specialize geographically, or by size of company, industry and/or type of position. It depends on the recruiters and their experience."

"There's really a lot to know about the industry, isn't there?" commented Ann.

"Yes," Chris said, "there is a lot to know. Most people don't realize it. I certainly didn't when I first got into the business. As I said earlier, recruiting seems like a fairly simple business, just matching people with jobs and with companies. However, there's so much more to it. Hopefully today's meeting helps you understand the industry a little more!"

"It does," said Raj, "especially for me, having just moved to Canada! Thanks so much for helping me understand the business."

Chris said, "No problem at all."

"I've heard that recruiters sometimes post job advertisements that don't exist just to build their database... does that really happen?" asked Ann.

Chris responded, "Well, I have heard that also. Generally the answer is no. I've worked with many recruiters over the years and, in my experience, recruiters are fairly busy people trying to find candidates for their open jobs. They are really focused on trying to work those open positions without trying to get candidates for jobs that don't exist. However, there are situations where recruiters know that their clients will have staffing needs for certain positions ahead of time, even though they don't have a confirmed order as yet. For example, where they know a client has specific needs through certain periods of the year. In those cases, recruiters may post positions that don't technically exist at that moment, knowing that the need will be there in the near future. Does that help?"

"Yes," replied Ann.

Chris asked, "Any other questions about the recruiting industry or what recruiters do?"

"I think you've covered quite a bit and I need to get home," said Ann, looking at her watch. Raj and Carlos nodded.

Ann asked if Chris would meet with them again and he agreed. The three scheduled another meeting the following Wednesday afternoon, again at 5:30 p.m.

CHRIS' THREE POINTERS:

1. Recruiters are paid by companies to help them find employees; you should rarely, if ever, have to pay a recruiter to help you find a position.

2. Staffing agencies, employment agencies, and recruiting firms all generally mean the same thing.

3. Recruiters typically don't write resumes. You can speak with a resume writer or coach who can help you with preparing your resume.

CHAPTER FIVE

"A RECRUITER WHO DOESN'T INTERVIEW?!"

As Ann, Carlos and Raj sat down in Chris' boardroom for their second meeting, Chris showed them a gift that had been given to him by one of the associations at which he had recently spoken. It was two tickets for an upcoming symphony show. Chris didn't really enjoy the symphony, so he offered the tickets to anyone who wanted them. Ann asked to have them so she could go with a friend, as Carlos and Raj weren't interested.

Chris explained that, as a recruiter, people always want to know about the industry and are regularly asking him to present at meetings, dinners, and other functions. Chris enjoyed speaking to any audience, regardless of the industry, the level of audience or even the seniority of the group since he enjoyed meeting new people.

Chris noted that he's asked to do presentations on various topics, such as networking, trends in the recruiting industry and tips on finding jobs. Chris added that a lot of the attendees at his presentations who are working are sometimes afraid to talk about their own job search since they didn't want word to somehow get back to their bosses – as such, they would approach him later with questions.

Ann thanked Chris for the tickets and Carlos jumped right in with a question. "You talked last week about your responsibilities as a recruiter, but can you talk a little more about how you find candidates for your clients?" he asked.

"Well…," Chris began, "there are many ways recruiters find people. We advertise our positions and get responses to our ads, we search for people in resume databases, and we get referrals from other people, including from other job seekers we have met. We also get referrals from people that we have placed before. When it comes to resume databases, we search for people based on salary, location, keywords and anything else that we can search on a resume. We have access to literally hundreds of thousands of resumes at our fingertips. It's just a matter of finding the right candidates for each position. There's an expression in the recruiting industry – 'Every Saucer has a Cup'. It means that everyone has a match somewhere – it's just finding the right match for each person to each position."

"Do you have a preference on where you find candidates?" asked Raj.

"It really depends on the position," Chris said. "My preference is to get a candidate through some kind of a referral. Generally, I find that if someone is referred to me, they will be a more trusted candidate than if I just find someone from a resume database. This is because there's a bit of trust. However, it always comes down to the person involved as I've also been referred poor candidates who have let me down."

"How do you find your clients?" asked Ann.

"I get my clients in a number of ways," said Chris. "I've found some clients through referrals from existing contacts and through relationships that are developed with people. We get companies that contact us as they've heard about our services and they have a staffing requirement. Sometimes one hiring manager refers another hiring manager within their organization and suggests they call us. My actual favourite way of getting clients is to just call companies and ask if they have any staffing needs I could help them with."

"I couldn't do that," chuckled Carlos.

"It sounds so much like a sales person," added Ann.

"There's no doubt that you need to have a bit of a sales mindset if you're going to be a recruiter," said Chris. "I actually prefer the sales and business development side of the recruiting business. I try to help companies improve themselves on the staffing side and I like to advise them as to how to find the best possible staff. Similar to job seekers, a lot of clients that I deal with don't have an idea of what the market is, what to pay staff, or what questions to ask in an interview with candidates. Sometimes they don't know what recruiters really do other than to help them find staff. I don't really do any interviews anymore."

Carlos asked, "A recruiter who *doesn't* interview?!"

"That is correct," smiled Chris. "I occasionally still interview some job seekers - usually people who have been referred to me by a good friend or contact. Interviewing candidates helps me maintain a good idea of the job market, understand changes in compensation levels, and identify any trends that I can share with my clients. I stopped doing a lot of interviews a couple of years ago. I don't actually like interviewing candidates."

Chris continued, "Typically, there are three types of recruiters:

- *Business Development* – this type of recruiter works with companies and networks to find companies looking for staff, but doesn't typically do any interviewing or sourcing of candidates; sales is the main focus for this role.

- *Interviews Candidates* – this type of recruiter primarily interviews candidates and finds people for open positions, but has limited contact with clients. This kind of recruiter typically likes dealing only with candidates.

- *Blend of Business Development and Interviewing* – this type of recruiter is known as running a '360 degree' desk – that is, they deal with all sides by finding clients, working on open positions, searching for and interviewing candidates and managing their clients.

Recruiters will fall into one of these three categories."

Raj asked, "How would I know which type of recruiter I might be dealing with?"

Chris responded, "You won't know unless you ask them."

"Won't they be offended if someone asked them?" Raj asked.

Chris replied, "No, they'll just let you know what their focus is and generally they'll be glad you asked so that they can clarify their role and manage your expectations. In fact, most job seekers won't even know to ask that question, so by asking you'll indicate that you have an understanding of the recruiting industry."

Raj commented, "I'm really surprised that you don't even like to interview candidates given the industry that you're in!"

"Yes, it's true," said Chris. "As I've gained more experience in the industry, I've realized there are certain responsibilities that I like to do and some that I don't like to do. People change what they want to do through the course of their careers and that's no different for me. In my career, I've interviewed on average eight to ten people a week, for 50 weeks a year for 17 years. That's about 7,000 to 8,000 interviews over the years and that's a lot of interviews! And when you meet that many people, you kind of get to know the different types of people. For example, there are introverts, extroverts, technical people, professional ones, ones that give red flags, etc. I suppose I'm just tired of doing interviews!" laughed Chris.

Tales from the Recruiter

"What do you mean by candidates who give you red flags?" asked Ann.

"Well, fairly frequently, a candidate tries to mislead a recruiter," explained Chris. "Maybe they think we're stupid, we won't check the facts or we'll overlook something. They might do this in different ways that will give me a red flag about them. A red flag is something about the job seeker that might cause me concern. For example, they might tell me that they're earning a certain salary which doesn't seem right because it's way over market or based on other people that I've interviewed at that company it just doesn't make sense. Or when I ask them who they report to or ask them for references, they hesitate. They might tell me that they will only give me that information when there's a position available. At that point, I'm usually not planning on calling the references when I first meet them anyways - I just want to see how they handle that question. Why are they being secretive about who they reported to? Also, are they giving me their friends and co-workers as references, or are they giving me their bosses?"

Chris continued, "Candidates who give me their friends or co-workers as references either don't know that they're not as important to recruiters or I suspect they're trying to hide something. A reference should be someone you reported to, not a friend or a co-worker. Friends always have good things to say about their friends! Or sometimes a candidate mysteriously doesn't remember the company's phone number where they worked for many years or their boss' name. Sometimes they don't want to sign our application form, which gives us permission to check references or to do a credit check. All of these, for me, are possible red flags from a candidate that makes me want to investigate further by asking more questions."

"Sounds like you should be a detective!" suggested Ann.

Chris responded, "When I started in the recruiting industry I really didn't know what I was doing. I trusted people a lot more than I do now. If someone told me how much they were earning, what their responsibilities were or what their title was, I would just take their word for it that they were telling me the truth. Now, years later, I'm much more skeptical about what people tell me and consider someone 'guilty until proven innocent'. I know that's not the legal system's way of doing things, but when it comes to sending candidates to my clients I need to be careful that I'm sending the best people available on the market. My reputation is on the line."

"I'm always on alert, not just when I'm meeting a job seeker for a first interview, but also through the entire process of placing a candidate," Chris continued. "Candidates might think that once they make it through a first interview with a recruiter that they don't need to worry about them anymore. Experienced recruiters will look at a candidate's behaviour throughout the entire interview process. For example, last year I met a candidate who I thought was a good candidate for one of my client's positions. He told me he was working with a big bank downtown. We agreed to meet during his lunch hour. When I interviewed him I thought he was a good candidate. When I set up a telephone interview for him the following week with my client, he told me he was on vacation but that he could be reached at home. I became suspicious when he said he could be reached at home for a second telephone interview with the client the following week, since that would mean that he was going to be on vacation at home for two consecutive weeks. While someone taking two consecutive weeks of vacation isn't impossible, it's generally not that common for people to do when it doesn't involve going out of town for at least part of their vacation. So I blocked my phone number, called the bank that he said he was working at and asked for him, but the receptionist didn't have him on the company's directory. Given the size of the bank, I wanted to give him the benefit of the doubt, just in case he worked at another location or division of the company. So I called him and asked him again if he was still working at the bank and he told me that he was. I told him that I called his work but they didn't have him on the company directory. He said that he didn't know why that would be."

"Can't wait to see where this is going...," remarked Carlos.

Chris smiled, "I told him that for me to continue to represent him with my client I needed at least one of three things to move forward:

(a) His direct phone number or his extension at the bank that I could call and hear his voice;
(b) Someone at the bank who would confirm that he was still working there; or
(c) A copy of his most recent pay stub from the bank.

He became very aggressive and asked me if I did this with all my candidates and told me that no other recruiter had ever asked him for any of this information. I told him that I didn't do this with all candidates that I met, but I had reason to believe that he was no longer working at the bank and that any of the three things that I had asked for would alleviate my concerns. He told me that if that was the case he would remove himself from the running as a candidate for the position."

"So he took himself out of the running?" asked Carlos.

"Yes," said Chris, "if he wasn't trying to hide anything, I'm sure he would have gladly given me any of those three items I asked for. I let my client know of my findings and recommended that they not move forward with the candidate. My client thanked me for finding this information out and sharing it with them. They also stopped pursuing him as a candidate for their job. The funny thing is that he was an excellent candidate for the position and had he been honest with me up-front, he probably would have got the job!"

"And so he never got another interview?" asked Carlos.

"No," Chris said, "and that's just the tip of the iceberg. I've had so many people lie to my face it's not funny anymore. They lie about the languages they speak, where they live, what they earn, what their responsibilities are or what dates they worked at a company. And that's just the start. As in the case with the gentleman I just mentioned, they'll lie about whether they're still working with a company or not. I'm not sure why candidates especially seem to want to lie about whether they are or are not still working with a company because it's such an easy thing for recruiters to find out whether it's fact or not. Many times they'll lie about their education. For example, early in my career I had a candidate put 'NCMA' after his name at the top of his resume. When I asked him what it meant he said 'Non-Certified Management Accountant'. Since I was still fairly green in the industry, I asked him what that meant as I thought it was some kind of special designation. He explained to me that he had never completed his Certified Management Accountant (CMA) designation, so he thought it would be appropriate to put 'NCMA' on his resume. I almost broke out laughing. I thought to myself that I should have 'N-Doctor' on my resume since I never became a doctor!"

Everyone broke out in laughter.

Chris laughed, "I tell you, if I had a penny for each time someone lied to me, I could retire."

"Wow, I can't believe people lie so much," said Ann.

Chris continued, "I've read a lot of different articles and it seems that the statistics are pretty high about people lying, especially whenever the job market is weak. My suggestion is to always be 100% honest with recruiters. You can never go wrong being honest. I've seen job seekers say and do a lot of weird things over the years. Even if you think that recruiters or companies will look negatively on you if you tell the truth about something, it will be worse if you get found out for lying about something later. You might get terminated from your job – I've seen that happen many times."

Everyone looked at each other and nodded their heads.

The discussion continued for another 10 minutes about candidates who gave Chris red flags and soon after the four decided to end their meeting.

Since everyone felt that the meetings were helpful and they were all enjoying the discussions, the four agreed to continue to meet weekly, every Wednesday at 5:30 p.m.

CHRIS' THREE POINTERS:

1. Recruiters use many resources to help them find candidates for jobs.

2. There are different types of recruiters – those that interview only, those that work with clients only, or those that do a blend of both.

3. Be honest with recruiters; experienced recruiters will be on the lookout for anything that might give them a red flag about you.

CHAPTER SIX

"WHAT'S WRONG WITH MY RESUME?"

As the four gathered for their weekly meeting, the discussion quickly turned to resumes and the challenges with writing them.

Raj began, "I have put in many hours updating my resume, including making sure there are no spelling or grammatical mistakes. Many people have given me advice on what to include in my resume, such as my accomplishments and education, and what to exclude, such as my birth date and religion. I keep changing my resume because everyone always has different recommendations for me, but I'm still not getting any interviews. So what's wrong with my resume?"

"Ann and Carlos – do you have this problem?" asked Chris.

Ann replied, "I just don't even know where to start with my resume, so Raj's question is good!"

Carlos said, "I have a resume that I update when I need to, but since I'm not really looking for a position, I don't worry about it too much."

"Fair enough," said Chris. "Well, let's talk about some ideas regarding resumes since it is always a big topic. I know many people who focus so much on making their resume perfect that they forget the end goal of getting a job. I heard a coach speak a year ago and he said that you should allocate about 30 hours of time to get your resume to the level required for recruiters. I think the amount of time it takes to put together a resume depends on the level of the person. For example, someone working as a shipper in a warehouse should take less time to do their resume than someone who is president of a company since their responsibilities will differ so much. Regardless, I think 30 hours is excessive. Putting together a two page document detailing your experience shouldn't take you that long, although I do realize that there could be quite a bit of behind the scenes work to get it right."

"You want to spend enough time that you're comfortable that your resume is an appropriate representation of your experience and accomplishments," explained Chris. "People have asked me my thoughts about having more than one resume. I usually tell them that their background is their background, meaning they can't really change what they've done in their work, their titles, what their responsibilities were in their positions, the dates of when they were with those companies, etc. This is factual information. The only thing they can change is their 'Objective' statement at the top of their resume. This objective statement tells the reader what type of position the job seeker is looking for, but it should still be within the same area of expertise that they're familiar with. For each of you, you can tailor that objective to the position that you're applying for. I think people spend way too much time worrying about their resumes than thinking about their job search. They spend hours debating the layout, the font, the format, the italics, the wording, the underlines, etc. Then they ask someone for advice and then they change everything again. I feel that a resume is only a way of opening the door to get in, but you can't forget to knock on the door to get in. I find the people who spend more time networking with people tend to get the best jobs and hear about more opportunities – the resume is an afterthought in a lot of those cases."

"I've received so much advice on my resume from so many different people," said Raj. "I've changed it many times, trying to adapt to the local way, based on what different people have told me."

Chris explained, "I always say that if you ask 100 people, including recruiters, coaches, friends, family and co-workers, to give feedback about the same resume, you'll get 100 different suggestions. It's enough to make someone go crazy. My suggestion is that you listen to what people recommend and then, based on your own personal preference, make your own conclusion about what you should have in there. Obviously, someone who is in the recruiting industry is going to be in a position to generally give you better advice since they're in the business. Keep in mind though, recruiters aren't professional resume writers. As such, they aren't necessarily the ones who know how to put the resumes together perfectly. However, they do know what their clients look for so they know how to position resumes in the best light. There are also resume writers who prepare resumes for a living and those people are very good resources. They are experienced in writing resumes and they know resume formats, effective words and sentences to use, etc. Generally speaking, take advice from people that are in the job industry more than from people who don't really know what they're talking about. Ask for assistance but use your own discretion as to what properly reflects you, your background, and your personality. If one of you had a graphic design background I would recommend that your resume reflect more of an artistic style, perhaps with fonts and styles that represent a graphic design type of person."

"I do spend way too much time on my resume," said Raj, "but I keep second-guessing myself as to whether I'm doing it right or not."

"There's no one way to write a resume," said Chris. "There are lots of different ways. I thought you would be asking about resumes at some point so I printed off these handouts for each of you. The first handout (*Appendix 1*) gives you some general points on what your resume should have. The second and third handouts give you different types of resumes. There are generally two types of resumes: chronological and functional. The chronological resume (*Appendix 2*) is the most common type – probably 90 to 95% of the people use this format and they should. The functional resume (*Appendix 3*) is for people who tend to have more contracts, or have several positions that duplicate in responsibilities and experience. You can see the differences between these two formats."

"So you think the three of us should be using a chronological resume?" asked Ann.

"Yes," Chris answered, "just stick to mainstream style resumes and you should be fine. I've been looking at resumes for 17 years now and, really, nothing has changed other than the words. The styles are pretty similar from when I got into the industry and I don't really expect things to change that radically in the next decade either even with the speed that the world changes!"

"The tips in this first handout are great. Any other tips on the resume you'd suggest?" asked Carlos.

"Well, I would just make your resume easy to read," said Chris. "Make the letters big enough so that it's easy for the reader. Some people try to squeeze so many words on a page and then they think they should make it as small as possible to get all the words in there to not go over two pages. Leave a lot of white space around the sides and at the top. Keep in mind that there is no 'perfect resume', just like there's no 'perfect boss', 'perfect company', 'perfect spouse, etc. Think about the substance of your resume and does it answer questions such as:

- What is it you want the reader to know about you?
- What experience do you have that is relevant to the position that you're applying for?
- Are the company names that you worked at there?

- Are the titles of the positions that you had on there?
- Are the dates clear of when you worked at those companies?
- Is the resume factually correct?

Whoever is receiving your resume won't see you in person, so you want to get your background across as quickly as possible."

"What about accomplishments?" asked Ann.

"Good question, Ann," said Chris. "You should definitely include some accomplishments in your resume. For example, something that you did that saved the company money or increased revenues, how you improved a process to save time, or how you were involved in a project and what the result was."

"How many resumes do recruiters get each day?" asked Carlos.

"Sometimes, literally hundreds," replied Chris.

Carlos, Raj and Ann gasped. "That's incredible," said Carlos.

"Yes and it's tough going through them," said Chris. "As such, recruiters who have been in the business for a long time learn to quickly skim through resumes to spot candidates who have the background that they're looking for. They can generally also find spelling and grammatical errors quite quickly. That's why you need to make sure that the main points are clear and concise. Make sure the important keywords are in your resume – what industries you've worked in, what systems you've used, etc. Recruiters skim for those keywords. Get to the point quickly and don't spend too much time with all kinds of fancy words. You will be called in for an interview if you have the background a recruiter is looking for."

"What if you think you're a great candidate for a position for which you've sent in your resume and you haven't been called in for an interview?" asked Ann.

"The world isn't perfect," said Chris. "Maybe the recruiter somehow never received your resume. Some clients have also told me that for some positions they receive so many resumes that they only have time to review the first batch of resumes that they receive. They take the chance that a 'perfect candidate' isn't in a later bunch of resumes. As such, to answer your question Ann, if you really feel you are a great candidate for the position and you haven't heard from anyone after a few days, follow-up with the company to make sure they at least received your resume. Find out who the recruiter or contact is or who the position reports to and call them to make sure that they at least have it. You don't need to say anything else – just ask them if they're sure that they've received it. If the conversation continues from there, just go with it. You might be able to get an interview!"

"What if I don't know who the contact is?" asked Ann.

"Do some research," replied Chris. "Call the company. Ask questions. Do some internet searches. Find out. If you really want the job and you're qualified for it, you should make the effort."

"What if the recruiter gets turned off because I contacted them?" asked Ann.

"If you're a good candidate for a position, they'll be happy that you followed up," said Chris. "If you're really not that appropriate for the position, don't bother. For example, if you don't have at least 80% of the skill requirements needed for the position I wouldn't try to pursue it. However, if you have over 80% of the skills needed for the position and you're a good match, with similar and relevant skills for a position, make sure to contact them. You never know – they may not have had time to review your resume or they never received it. One other thing I should mention is that if you're thinking about making a switch to a different career, it's probably not the most appropriate to send your resume to a recruiting firm asking them to help you with a career change, such as moving from accounting to sales or customer service to human resources. Recruiters in recruiting firms work to find candidates for their clients that have the backgrounds similar to what their clients look for. Square to square. Apple to apple. If a client of a recruiting firm is looking for a 'circle', and they're paying them significant dollars to find them a 'circle', the recruiting firm needs to find them a 'circle', not a 'square', 'rectangle' or anything else. If you want to make a career change, you need to really learn to network, which is a totally separate topic. Do you know what I mean?"

"I get it," nodded Carlos.

"Should we put a picture of ourselves on our resume?" asked Ann.

Chris replied, "You should do whatever you feel is best to increase your chances of getting an interview. Remember, a resume is only intended to get you in the door. Will a picture of yourself on the resume help or hurt your chances? That's what you need to think of. Everyone feels differently. It's what you feel most comfortable with and what you think will help you get in the door. I presented last year to a room full of recruiters and asked them what their preference was when reviewing resumes – half said they liked resumes with pictures on them and half said they didn't."

Ann smiled.

"What about gaps in my resume?" asked Carlos. "A few years ago I took a year off to go travelling. Should I just leave that time period blank? I'm sure it's the same for a parent who quits their job and stays at home with the children for a few years. What do we do in that situation?"

"Depending on the situation," said Chris, "I would indicate that on your resume. For example, 'Travelling for one year' or 'Child care for three years' or something along those lines will make sense. Recruiters like to see continuity and will always ask about gaps so I feel it's best to indicate it up-front."

"That makes sense," said Carlos.

Chris added, "So, to answer Raj's original question of what's wrong with his resume, there's probably nothing technically wrong with it. It's probably that he doesn't have the relevant experience, especially for the positions that he's applying for. Raj, I would suspect the people to whom you're sending your resume are receiving it, but you're not meeting the requirements of their position and that's why you're not hearing back from them. You don't have experience in Canada and that is always a tough challenge for New Canadians."

"How do I get around this problem then, Chris?" asked Raj.

Chris answered, "You may need to find other ways. You could volunteer to get some Canadian experience. You might have to take something lesser than what you're qualified for. You're going to have to network and meet people. You're going to have to make as many contacts as you can. You're going to have to think of Plan B, or Plan C – what happens if you don't get that dream job? And while you're doing that, you're going to have to stay positive, not get down, and be humble. There are going to be people less smart than you who are going to get positions that you're more qualified for. Canada is a bit ruthless that way until you can get that one break and start proving yourself. There are people who are going to move up the corporate ladder faster than you, even though you have more experience. That's just the way the job market in Canada seems to work. And the longer things may take to find a position, the more you may get down, but on the outside you're going to have to be as positive as ever. The moment you let other people see that you're down, the tougher it's going to become for you. No one wants to hire someone who is negative. In the extreme situation where you can't find a job, you might be forced to take a 'survival' job or you might consider going back to India if you had to – I've seen that happen many times."

"Yes, some of the people at the employment centre that I've been to have taken a survival job just to make ends meet," commented Raj.

"It is reality, Raj," said Chris. "I'd rather be honest with you as to what I've seen from people over the years. I met a guy from Jamaica last week at a job fair who had a great accounting job in Jamaica but moved to Canada with the promise of prosperity and a better life. I'm not sure who exactly told him that it would be easy in Canada or what research he had done beforehand about living here, but the reality is he came with high expectations but now he was working in construction just to make money."

"I don't want to get to that point," said Raj.

"As I mentioned," said Chris, "if you're struggling to find something Raj, just stay positive, be humble, or do work that is below what you're capable of just to get experience. Volunteer if necessary. Do whatever it takes."

"That's sad for people new to Canada," said Ann. "I didn't know stuff like that was going on."

"Yes, unfortunately it goes on all around us," said Chris. "And one other point is that this doesn't just apply to people from other countries – it applies to people here also. For example, many students graduate from programs in university or college and expect well-paying jobs in their fields only to find out they can't get something in the same line of work because they might lack the qualifications, skills, experience, maturity, presentation or communication skills, or the jobs just don't exist for people in the program they just graduated from. This also happens with more experienced people where their skills are just not in demand anymore. Those people might have to change directions in their careers and take something that is lower than what they were used to. There are many people in Canada that are not willing to do work that they feel is beneath them. So they sit and wait. They become more negative. Their expectations become higher, as if someone will come and offer them a tremendous job. Their resume becomes filled with part-time jobs. Their career stalls. It's not good."

"This is a bit of a sad meeting," said Carlos.

"We should all be aware of the reality," said Chris. "If each of you can talk to your friends about these situations hopefully it may help someone somewhere. Be compassionate to people from overseas like Raj, because I see it every day."

Ann, Raj and Carlos nodded.

"Any other tips on resumes?" asked Ann.

"It's always good to have your resume up-to-date," said Chris. "If your responsibilities change, make sure to add that to your resume while it's fresh in your mind. It's easier to remember when it's kept current as you go than years later. You also never know when an unexpected opportunity might come up."

"Thanks for all your help," said Ann.

"And your honesty also," said Raj.

"No problem," said Chris, "I know it's getting late, but how about I change it up and give you some funny stories about resumes?"

Ann, Carlos and Raj smiled. "Sure."

Chris said, "Ok, well here are some amusing things that I remember seeing on resumes that people wrote (*spelling mistakes on purpose*):

- Extracurricular work – 'Tudored English class'
- Education – 'Had 16th highest mark out of a class of 20'
- Other Interests – 'Smoke a pack of cigarettes daily'

- Computer Skills – 'Can typ 32 words per minut'
- Objective – 'To get a job'

They all shared a laugh.

"It is amazing what people include on their resumes," sighed Chris.

At that point, the four finished their weekly meeting and agreed to meet again the following week.

CHRIS' THREE POINTERS:

1. Have a resume ready at all times even if you're not actively looking – you never know what opportunities might come up.

2. Most people should be using a chronological resume, not a functional resume.

3. Apply to and follow-up on positions that you have at least 80% of the requirements asked for.

CHAPTER SEVEN

"WHAT SHOULD I BE EARNING?"

Raj, Ann and Carlos were finding that their meetings with Chris very useful. It gave them a chance to listen to stories and ideas about recruiting that they wouldn't otherwise know. Chris also loved sharing stories about the industry because this was how others would learn the things to do and not to do in their respective job searches.

Everyone in the working world always has a hilarious memory about something that happened to them, a co-worker or a boss. In the recruiting world, it's much the same, although you get to hear a lot more stories than average.

Chris began the week's meeting by recollecting the most amusing story he remembered within the recruiting world. He recalled with a grin, "I think the funniest story I ever came across was the time when a candidate went for an interview through my previous recruiting firm. The candidate was sent out to an interview with one of our bigger clients, and the candidate was fairly inexperienced. The interview was scheduled late in the day due to the candidate's work schedule. Somehow, after the interview ended around 6:00 that night, the doors to where she was let out into the hallway by the interviewer locked automatically - she couldn't get out of the corridor, she was stuck between two locked doors and didn't have a cell phone."

"So what did she do?" asked Ann.

"Well, she did the only thing she could do," explained Chris, "and that was to pull the fire alarm!" Everyone broke out in laughter.

"The fire trucks came to this large tower only to find out that this candidate had been locked in. It was too funny, although the firefighters were not amused. I'm sure it wasn't fun for the candidate to be in that situation either, but every time I think about this story I just get such a kick out of it! So many stories in this industry, someone could think they're made up!" Everyone chuckled some more.

Chris asked, "So, what questions do you have for me this week?"

Ann said, "Chris, one of my biggest questions is: What should I be earning? Is there a place I should go where I can get salary information or find out what people are making? It always seems that anyone who interviews me asks me what I'm looking for but I never really know what to say or where to get the information from and the interviewer holds all the cards. Can you give me any suggestions?"

Chris started, "You know, Ann, that's a great question. It's also one of the most common questions I get asked from people. Let's spend this week's meeting talking about that. Unfortunately the job market is not like the real estate market, where you can search very easily for what houses are selling. With jobs, it's not so easy. For the most part, companies like to keep what they're paying their staff confidential. Similarly, people don't like to share what they earn, even with their friends and family."

"There are a number of ways that you can find out what jobs pay and what you should be earning, and I'll go through a few of these. Part of the difficulty in finding out salaries is that it takes time and a lot of research and it's not an exact science. Salary ranges depend on a lot of factors, including market conditions, geography, supply and demand for positions, the economy, how much a candidate needs a job, and how much a company needs a candidate. It generally follows the laws of supply and demand where the more supply of candidates there are for a particular position, the lower the salary that a company needs to pay. The lower the supply of candidates there are for a particular position, the more a company will need to pay to compete against other companies for the same talent. In addition, it also depends on what companies have as their budgets. Also, sometimes companies work off a 'salary grid' where they have certain salary ranges for certain positions in their companies."

"What drives the supply of candidates?" asked Carlos.

"It really depends on many factors," explained Chris, "such as the educational programs, immigration, history of an area, pay ranges, number of graduating students in a particular program and the demographics of a certain region. Those are just some of the many elements that can go into determining the supply of candidates."

"What drives the demand for candidates?" asked Raj.

Chris replied, "Demand for candidates is a different set of factors from supply, such as how a particular company or industry is doing, where a company is set up geographically relevant to where potential workers live, what services or products are in demand, etc. As such, you can imagine that there are a lot of factors for both supply and demand. The trick to earn the most money is to be in the most demand when you know there is the least supply."

"For example," Chris explained, "if there are a high number of people going into school for human resources, for example, your best bet is to avoid that area. However, obviously if you really love HR, you'll do better at it than someone who doesn't like it, but it might not pay the most if there's a high supply of people in it. If someone is just going into college or university, it's hard to know what's going to be hot in three or four years. What usually happens is that if there's a sector that is hot, many people start getting into it, taking courses and switching careers. This drives down salaries for that particular area in the following two to three years. I would suggest specializing in an area which you love the most because, even if it doesn't pay the most, the fact that you love your job or your career will make up for any reduced earnings."

Carlos, Raj and Ann nodded.

"I know so many people who are in a job or a career that they just fell into without doing a lot of research beforehand," continued Chris. "This could be because their parents wanted them to get into it or maybe they thought they would like it. But they really don't like it, let alone love it – they are just going through the motions. There are all kinds of examples of these people with all types of backgrounds. There's the recent college graduate who went into commerce because he thought he liked business but found out he hated it. The 45-year old sales manager who really doesn't like managing people. The 30-year old accountant who really doesn't like accounting. These people hate what they do in their chosen career but make good money at it; overall they are still unhappy. They go to work unhappy. They come home unhappy. Their whole life becomes miserable and all they do is complain to their spouses at night about how much they hate their jobs. They didn't do enough research because they thought they would learn to like it or they wanted to make their parents happy. It's not always about salary and overall compensation."

"I've met many people like that," said Carlos.

"I myself didn't really know what I wanted to do, but when I got into recruiting I realized this was a career and profession that I really loved doing. I just fell into it and got a bit lucky, but I did do quite a bit of research in the industry and the profession before I started in it. I was making a career change myself from accounting and I wanted to make sure I was doing the right thing, so I spoke with a lot of other recruiters about how they made the switch in their careers, what they liked about the industry and what motivated them."

"How do you go about finding out what to do when making a career change, Chris?" asked Ann.

"Well, I would suggest to anyone either looking to get into a profession or work in a certain role to ask people who are there now," Chris suggested, "Ask them questions such as:

- What do they enjoy about their role?
- What kind of person is successful in that role?
- What kind of compensation might someone be able to earn?

Doing this kind of research helps to uncover what the role entails and if it's a potential match for them. People spend more time comparing the cost of different canned soup brands at the grocery store than they do on figuring out what might be the best thing to do in their careers."

"Now," expanded Chris, "to answer your question Ann, let me give you some further direction as to where you can go to find out about how much you should be earning. First of all, you can check out salary guides. There are many of them available and you should be able to find many of them by doing a few internet searches. These guides have salary ranges for hundreds of positions, including pretty much every type of role. These guides are useful for job seekers. In fact, I also let my clients know about these guides when they ask me for salary information."

"For your clients also?" asked Carlos.

"Yes," said Chris, "employers can use these guides to determine salary ranges for their positions within their geographic area. Job seekers can use these guides to compare, contrast and set personal benchmarks. The information in these guides varies in regards to how they determine their data. Some commonly used resources include surveys of employees as well as reports from human resource professionals."

"What other tools would you use if you were us?" asked Ann.

"I would ask recruiters at recruiting firms who specialize in your area of expertise." suggested Chris. "You can certainly ask me, but Ann you might also want to ask a few recruiters that specialize in accounting. Carlos, you might ask a recruiter or two who specialize in IT recruitment. Recruiters are privy to a vast range of information for various industries and positions. Contacting recruiters who regularly place candidates in your area of expertise to ask them about salary ranges for a particular position can be very helpful. They would be able to give you a benchmark for salary ranges for people with similar backgrounds."

Chris continued, "It is also important for you to consider the value of the whole employment package, especially if you get a job offer. That is, don't just look at base salary, but also think of any and all bonuses, commission, benefit plans, vacation entitlement, matching contributions to any pension plans, vacation time, commuting time, parking costs, etc. This is important when you are looking at both what you're making and comparing it to a new offer. Doing so will help you decide on what the total compensation plan is, not just what the base salary is."

"This is good stuff – what else can you suggest Chris?" asked Carlos.

Chris smiled, "Asking peers or friends who have similar backgrounds to you is always a good idea. "I know that many people don't want to discuss salary and compensation with their friends. However, if it's just to share information, people are usually open to discussing general salary ranges for positions."

"I never thought about all these points," Ann remarked.

"Yes Ann," said Chris, "these are just some ideas for you, but you do have to do your homework. When you meet with a recruiter they will ask you your salary expectations and you need to be ready to answer. You need to think of what the market is for someone with your background, what you're currently making and whether you would leave your job for less money, more money or the same. I find that when I interview someone who has a good grasp of the salary they're looking for, they come across as more confident."

"What if I don't know?" asked Raj.

"I would suggest you answer with the minimum amount of what you're looking to get paid. What's your bottom line? You should be able to tell me 'Chris, don't bother calling me for positions below this salary or hourly rate because I won't be interested.' What is that number and that will be your answer. For example, you can say 'Chris, my minimum expectations are $X per year or $Y per hour' and leave it at that. There's nothing more that needs to be said."

"Very helpful," said Ann.

"Glad to help," said Chris. "Any other questions on what you should be making?"

Ann, Carlos and Raj looked at each other and shook their heads.

After a little more discussion, the four decided to end the week's meeting.

As Chris went to get his jacket, Ann, Carlos and Raj were quiet leaving the room. They were obviously thinking about what Chris had told them about salaries and realized they all needed to do some research.

CHRIS' THREE POINTERS:

1. Know what the demand and supply is for positions by speaking with recruiters.

2. Find out what positions are paying by looking at salary guides.

3. Determine the bottom compensation (annual salary or hourly rate) that you are looking for before meeting with recruiters.

CHAPTER EIGHT

"I HAVE NO EXPERIENCE - WHAT DO I DO?"

As the weekly meeting got started, Chris told the others that they had covered a lot of topics in the first few meetings. However, there was still so much to talk about regarding employment, job searching, recruiters, etc. There was never enough time to cover everything.

Even in a 17-year and counting career in recruiting, Chris pointed out that there was always something new that he himself learned. For example, how people think, changes in job search methodologies, organizations that were constantly changing their hiring processes and trends in what careers were hot or not.

The group decided that Raj should have the opportunity to ask questions at this week's meeting. Chris anticipated that Raj was going to ask him some tough questions, since he was new to Canada and he didn't have a lot of contacts.

Raj started, "As you know, Chris, I've been in Canada for only a few months and it looks like it's going to be a struggle to find a job. Back home, I had an excellent position where I was well-respected and had seniority. Here, I am treated as if I'm a nobody. I don't have any contacts or friends. When I was back home I was told that Canada was going to be a land of opportunity, but I am barely given a chance by anyone. There is a gap between the message announced and marketed in India and the real market here. Employers look at my resume and I think they just discard it because they see I don't have Canadian experience. I never get a call or even an acknowledgement from anyone. Basically, I have no experience here in Canada, but I have so much back home – what do I do?"

Chris nodded his head. He understood. He had heard the same story literally hundreds, if not thousands of times before Raj. He knew it was tough for someone starting a new life in Canada and that Canada can be unforgiving in many ways.

Chris started, "Raj, I understand what you're going through. I grew up here so I can't say I've been in your shoes before, but I've heard this question many times before you from job seekers who have immigrated to Canada over the years. I hear the same kind of questions from students who graduate from university or college and have no experience. They ask me 'How can I get a job if I don't have experience and how can I get experience if no one will give me a job?' I'm going to be brutally honest with you today and I hope that's ok?"

Raj nodded his head.

Chris continued, "Ann and Carlos - I would suggest you also pay attention to what I'm going to say because a lot of these principles apply to you also."

Ann and Carlos sat up in their chairs.

Chris started by telling some stories of clients. "To be honest with the three of you, I've seen all kinds of favouritism over the years. Some clients want a male in a certain position and some clients want females. Some organizations prefer younger employees in their organizations while some prefer older employees. Some want a woman who is married and has kids. Some want a woman who is older with grown up kids or is past their child-bearing years, so she won't go on maternity leave. I've seen examples of both favouritism and reverse favouritism. An example of the latter was when I met a manager in a large organization who was looking to hire someone for her department. She was a visible minority. She told me she didn't want another employee who was of the same visible minority as herself in her department. This was because her department already consisted of the same people as herself. She didn't want other employees and managers in the organization to think that she only hired people of her own visible minority."

Carlos, Raj and Ann blinked in disbelief.

Chris continued, "I've encountered clients who have wanted attractive young women in jobs, especially in a receptionist role. I've met other clients who don't want anyone to challenge their authority, so they want someone introverted and who won't rock the boat. These are the things that you won't ever see on a job description. People won't talk about these things except behind closed doors. There will be candidates who don't get the job, but are perfectly qualified for the role and wonder why someone with less experience ends up getting hired."

"The good news is that when I meet my clients, I challenge them on why these discriminatory requirements exist. I ask them if they would still interview a candidate that didn't meet their discriminatory terms. Most of the time they will still interview candidates who meet the criteria and, in many cases, end up hiring someone that is not what they were originally limiting themselves to. There are, however, some clients who insist upon these discriminatory requirements. If they do, I won't work with them. I feel that if a client is so narrow-minded in their beliefs, then it's not worth working with them. However, I'm sure there are recruiters in Canada who will still work the search. Those recruiters are also opening themselves up to potential discrimination lawsuits by a job seeker."

Carlos asked, "Do these things happen a lot? Do companies really give you discriminatory requirements when you work with them? What percentage of the time?"

Chris elaborated, "Well, it does happen. I don't know the statistics off the top of my head because I've never analyzed them, but I would say I see some sort of discrimination at least 10-20% of the time."

Ann said, "That seems quite high."

"Yes, it is," replied Chris. "Also, it puts recruiters in a bit of an awkward situation because recruiters obviously want the placements and to earn the commission, but it could mean compromising their ethics. On the positive side, there are many companies that do want diversity in their organizations and they hire to get people with different experience – age, sex, ethnicity, etc. This broader base of employees tends to give those organizations more balanced teams. However, there are some companies that will post that they look for diverse backgrounds, but sometimes they don't really mean it when it comes to making job offers to candidates."

Carlos asked, "Any other things you see companies doing right or wrong?"

"Well," began Chris, "many times I've met with a company who has said to me 'We need to see skills one, two, three, four and five in a successful candidate and we are willing to pay a maximum of $X for the position - no ifs, ands or buts.' They tell me that if the candidates don't have those five skills in the given salary range, they don't want to see them. Usually it's an HR person who is putting such stringent criteria for the search because they have been told by the hiring manager within their organization that those are the requirements. However, most times the hiring manager will be flexible on something - perhaps the salary or one of the skills isn't truly required. I tell them I probably won't be able to find someone who has everything, because the person doesn't exist. I ask them what skills they can be flexible on. They tell me they can't really negotiate on anything. Weeks go by and I haven't been able to find someone, but regularly check in with them. They tell me they're still looking and for me to do the same. Now they might have multiple agencies working on the same search. Eventually, what do you think happens?"

Ann guessed, "They end up finding someone else?"

Chris said, "Yes, they do, but not with someone who has everything they were originally looking for. Usually I can find the resume of the person that they end up hiring and the successful candidate's experience is nothing close to what the initial five requirements were or is not within the salary range that they were offering. At least 50% of the time, the person was found through some kind of referral. Many times I will have known of the candidate, but I wouldn't have sent them to the client because they weren't a close enough match. I do try to get my clients to interview candidates who are close to what they're looking for, but ultimately it's up to the client to decide who they want to hire."

"When I speak with my contact at the organization," Chris continued, "the conversation goes something along the lines of the following:

Me: Thanks for letting me know that you hired a candidate for the role. I'm just wondering though… I had <the successful candidate's name> in my database and considered her, but she didn't have all the criteria that you told me you were looking for.

Client: Well, that's true, but she was referred to us by someone who works here. It's one of our employee's friends and we met her and thought she would be a good fit for the role.

Me: …not to belabour the point, since it sounds like things are finalized, but she doesn't have skills two, four and five that you mentioned to me that were required for this position. Also, as far as I know, she is about $5,000 to $10,000 more than what you told me the top end of your salary range was.'

Client: Yes, that's true Chris. Unfortunately the <fill in the blank here with president, line manager, department manager, controller, VP of IT, etc.> thought that she would be a good fit and that we could train her in the areas that she was deficient in. As for salary, we reviewed it to accommodate her higher salary expectations."

"Carlos, what is the moral of this story?" Chris asked.

"That who you know matters? And that just because you don't have all the skills required, doesn't mean you won't get hired, especially if you know someone? And the more people you know the better the chance of getting a job?" Carlos suggested.

Chris answered, "Yes, to all of the above! In many cases, who you know overrides any skills or experience that you might lack. I mean, they're not going to hire a security guard for a controller position, but if you're pretty close in qualifications for a position, you're going to have a huge advantage over anyone else, especially if you know someone personally and it's a referral."

"I guess you're suggesting to network as much as possible?" asked Raj.

"Yes!" replied Chris. "Let's talk about networking at next week's meeting because that's a big topic, okay?"

The others nodded.

Chris continued, "The point is that when it comes to searching for a job, knowing people makes a *huge* difference in whether you get a job or not. The more relationships you have with people and the stronger those relationships are the better chances you have of hearing about and landing a job. Who you know bypasses all the regular screening processes that are in place with companies when they are hiring someone. In fact, when I was 16 years old, my parents were able to get me a teller position at a major bank for the summer as a result of their friendship with a VP who worked there. It was a great summer job, but I didn't have any of the qualifications that they were looking for in the posting. In fact, to be honest with you, I had no relevant experience for that job. The only experience I had was delivering newspapers on Sundays to houses and apartments in the area where I lived. I didn't really want to rely on my parents for help in finding a job, but they were able to get me a job because of their relationship with that VP. It was as easy as that! I don't even think I had a resume at the time, let alone knew what a resume was!"

"Good story, Chris," chuckled Carlos.

"Thanks!" said Chris. "So Raj, what I would suggest is to form good relationships with people and look for opportunities that can get you in the door with a company. Here are some other tips I would suggest for you, Raj, and some of these tips both Ann and Carlos can also benefit from:

Post your resume online
Posting your resume on a job board increases your chances of being found by recruiters. Recruiters search resume databases by keyword, skills and location. They will contact you directly if they feel that your experience can match the position that they're looking to fill, even if you don't have the relevant local experience.

Take a position for which you are overqualified
I've seen many people rise in companies over the years because they were initially humble enough to take something less than what they were qualified for. Some see this as a sign of weakness; however, there are many advantages to doing so. Advantages include getting experience quickly, networking with others, showing what you can do and avoiding having your resume show a time gap between jobs.

Many people I know have 'stuck to their guns', waiting for a 'perfect' job, only to be disappointed that they can't get an equivalent job. They ultimately take something that is not even related to their field because they become desperate. Being a little humble works wonders. In your case Raj, this might be an option for you.

Work with a recruiting firm
Recruiting firms can help in your job search. It's good to include recruiters in your network as they may be aware of opportunities that are sometimes not advertised, but don't rely exclusively on them to help you find a position.

A good strategy is to make a connection with two to three specific recruiters who specialize in your area of expertise on a periodic basis, at least once a month if you are actively looking for a position. Let them know you're looking for a new job. Do not contact them every day though – doing so will actually work against you.

Get a mentor
There are usually some government programs that can match you up with a mentor. Contact your local government or ask someone you respect to be

your mentor to give you guidance in your search.

Ask for informational interviews
Make contact with professionals in companies within your area of expertise and ask them if they will give you information on how to help in your job search. When you connect with them, don't ask for an 'interview', but rather let them know that you're looking for information on ways they would suggest you should go about finding a job.

Go to job or career fairs
Job and career fairs happen all the time. Going to a job fair can be very informative to help you in your job search because you can meet local employers there, but don't expect that you will get a job directly at the fair. Bring lots of copies of your resume, hand them out to exhibitors and follow-up with them after the fair.

Start your own business
This may be difficult depending on factors such as your experience, your personality and your financial situation; however, if there's something you're qualified for that you can start even part-time, there is certainly opportunity to grow. Do something that you're familiar with and where you know that the current available services or products are lacking.

For example, if your background is in accounting, like Ann's, you could start up a small bookkeeping service. To keep your expenses as low as possible, you could work out of your home initially.

We'll talk about starting up a business in more detail another week because it does require more discussion then we have time for today.

Upgrade your skills/education
There are many schools, colleges and other educational institutions that offer courses to upgrade your skills. Taking a course, even if it is a night school course or part-time, can help you improve your chances in your job search as you can include this on your resume.

Get your international credentials evaluated
For Raj, getting your international credentials evaluated to determine your equivalent standing can be very useful. At a minimum, you will find out how your background equates to local standards and will give you an idea of where you might need to take courses to supplement your education.

Take a temporary position
Similar to the advantages of taking a position that you are overqualified for as I mentioned earlier, this option can get you some valuable experience and earn money in the meantime. Employers and recruiters will generally be more helpful to you if you start by saying you're willing to do anything right from the start (even if it is temporary).

Follow-up
If an employer grants you an interview, follow-up with a thank you note, and touch base periodically with them to see if any opportunities have come up, even if you didn't get the original position to which you applied."

"So, in conclusion," Chris explained, "there are a lot of things you can do, but some are not easy and will take a lot of work and time. You'll get rejected more than you'll get accepted. Reward yourself for any successes or accomplishments, even if they're small, to stay motivated. Don't get discouraged. Maintain a positive attitude throughout the process. It can be a tough road to find a job, but if you follow some, or all, of the suggestions that I've brought up today, you *will* hear about opportunities."

"This was great information, Chris," Raj said.

"Thanks, Raj!" said Chris. "There are lots of opportunities out there, but you can't wait for something to happen. You need to be proactive."

"So, we're talking about networking next week?" asked Ann.

"Yes, I think that would be a good topic for next week," said Carlos.

All agreed. The weekly meeting wrapped up and the four left the building.

CHRIS' THREE POINTERS:

1. Creating strong relationships with people will help overcome a lot of the 'lack of experience' objections.

2. Be proactive in your job search – there are lots of things you can do.

3. Be prepared to be rejected more than you'll be accepted when you're looking for a job.

CHAPTER NINE

"HOW CAN I NETWORK IF I DON'T KNOW ANYONE?"

As Chris, Raj, Ann and Carlos met up for their next weekly meeting Chris asked what each of them liked to do in their spare time.

Ann mentioned that she liked to spend a lot of time with family - including her many nieces and nephews. Raj mentioned that he liked to take drives with his family, explore parks, nature, and enjoyed bird-watching; he commented on the splendour of Canada's nature. Carlos talked about how he liked to play as many sports as he could. He periodically played either touch football, soccer or ball hockey with friends.

Ann asked Chris, "What do you like doing, Chris?"

Chris said, "Ann, I also like spending time with family on nice days. But, truth be told, I'm a bit of a workaholic. I really enjoy the work I do and, when I'm not doing something with my family, I'm doing something work-related. It could be that I'm at networking meetings, doing volunteer work that I do for various associations I belong to, or calling previous candidates I've interviewed to talk to them about their status. I always find things I enjoy that are work-related. I never have a shortage of things I can do, especially in the recruiting world."

Carlos asked, "Don't you take time off?"

"Yes, Carlos, I do. In fact, I probably take more time off than most people. I try to take at least one week off every three months or so, so I'll take about four weeks off a year, not including regular holidays that come up during the year. I'm one of those people that work hard but then schedule the time to relax also." Chris continued, "My favourite vacations are going to a beach or a resort with the family for a week and just completely shutting down – just reading books and maintaining a healthy relationship with my wife and family. It's important for me to get away from work and recharge my batteries. It helps me clear my mind and makes me think of the big picture. I actually find that I become more creative during that week off and find solutions to problems or ways to make my work or life more efficient. Sometimes solutions were right in front of me but I didn't see them because I was too busy. Someone once told me 'Don't major in the minors', meaning don't focus all your efforts on the small stuff. I find the longer the time between vacations, the more the small stuff becomes bigger issues for me and the more stressed out I get. For example, if I don't take a vacation over a long stretch, I find that something small like being stuck in traffic on my way to work will become more and more irritating. Or, when a short line up at the bank becomes a 10 minute wait I tend to get really frustrated. At that point, I know I'm getting '*squirrely*' and that's when I know I'm due for a vacation."

"Squirrely?" asked Raj. Ann and Carlos laughed.

"Yes," smiled Chris, "It's just a name for it that I came up with. I don't know if that's a real word or not, but it means when I get irritated over minor things. My stress level becomes a lot higher and my patience becomes a lot shorter. I'll have to look up that word in the dictionary some day! It's just important to take time off to recharge."

Ann said, "I think you're describing me right now, Chris. I am so stressed because of the amount of work I have and the lack of recognition I get. Many times my boss just drives me crazy in a meeting and I grit my teeth because I'm so annoyed at the things he does and says. Sometimes I just have to go for a walk for a few minutes to get away from it all, but it comes right back later that day."

Chris asked, "Ann, when was the last time you took a vacation?"

Ann responded, "A real vacation? Like what you're describing? It's been at least a couple of years. First of all, I can't afford to take a vacation and secondly, I can't get the time off from work. I think I'm pretty '*squirrely*' right now actually."

Chris noted, "Sounds like you might need a vacation more than you know. You need to ask for the time off and if you can't afford going away, just do stuff around the city. You don't need to go to a resort – it just sounds like you need to decompress. Stay at home if you have to, turn the phone off, don't check emails, and just read a couple of books or watch some movies. Visit places you don't normally go to. Go to a museum, see a show or do something to get your mind off work. Take a book and go to a park alone. I find that the '*squirrelier*' I get, the more days off it takes me just to decompress. For example, it might take me two to three days of not doing anything before I start feeling a little more relaxed if I'm really stressed out. By the seventh day of doing nothing, I feel totally recharged."

Ann said, "I'll have to speak to my boss to see if I can get the time off."

Chris said, "It's not a question of whether you can get the time off – it's a must! You have to emphasize to your boss that you need to take a vacation. Tell your boss that you're feeling overwhelmed. You might actually find that your boss might respect you more for asking for the time to recharge. You'll have a totally different outlook about your work and your life if you take my advice and take a week off to yourself. Don't take just a couple of days off either. Finish on the Friday afternoon, take the weekend, the next week and then the following weekend off. It should give you a solid nine free days without anything. You'll feel refreshed. You should do that too, Carlos, if you're feeling the same."

Carlos said, "You know, Chris, that's great advice, but I do that anyway. There are some times when I do feel that way, so I take time off. It definitely helps me look at my life and career differently."

Ann asked Carlos, "You knew this already?"

Carlos said, "Yes, I don't know where I learned it. Maybe it's from my parents or something. But time off is definitely important. There's a lot of stress in the work world and you need time off to make sure that the stress isn't going to be harmful."

Chris said, "I like to think of stress as an elastic. If you stretch that elastic to the point that it doesn't break it's fine; however, if you pull that elastic and it breaks you're in trouble. *A little* stretch is fine. *A lot* of stretch is dangerous. You have to manage your life and your work to make sure it's in balance. As soon as I take my vacation, I start scheduling my next vacation so I space the time apart. For me, three months is a good amount of time between vacations. I typically take a week off in March when the kids are off school, one when the kids finish school in June, the last week of the summer just before the kids go back to school, and then in December when work slows down. This schedule seems to keep me refreshed."

Ann said, "That's great advice. Thank you."

Chris said, "No problem, Ann. How did we get on to this topic, anyway?"

Everyone laughed.

Chris asked, "Who has a question this week?"

Raj said, "Remember Chris, we were going to talk about networking this week? Perhaps we can talk about that today? For me personally, the question would be how can I network if I don't know anyone?"

Carlos said, "I agree. I think I'm a pretty good networker, but I'm always open to hearing ideas to improve also. I know a lot of people but maybe we can go over a few tips."

Chris said, "Well, everyone can always be a better networker and there are always tips that people have. I think I'm a better than average networker, but I know I can improve as well. I'm happy to share some things I've learned over the years. Some of the things that I do might help you and maybe we can all share other success stories."

Raj said, "That would be very helpful."

"Well, first of all, Raj, you already know people." Chris reminded.

Raj responded, "No, I don't. I just moved here six months ago and haven't met anyone."

Chris said, "You do. What about the three of us? What about the host of the party where we met? Did you reconnect with him since the party?"

Raj shook his head.

Chris continued, "What about the people you meet who run the employment centres that you go to? What about the person who cuts your hair? What about your neighbours? What about…"

Raj interrupted, "I understand what you're getting at. I never really thought about those people as being able to help me. I wasn't thinking of them as being part of my network, and wasn't really comfortable asking for help from them. I was thinking of human resource people or managers at companies."

"Networking isn't about asking for help from people," said Chris, "it's about sharing information, asking what you can do to help them, finding out contacts that they know who are able to help you, etc. It's not about what they can do for you, but what you can do for them. Perhaps they have a problem that you can help them fix. It's asking people 'How can I help you?' before asking them for help."

Raj said, "I've always wanted to ask them if they can help me find a job, but I didn't want to lose their friendship."

Chris said, "First of all, I'd be surprised if someone wouldn't be your friend if you asked them to help you find a job. But secondly, networking isn't about asking someone for a job. It's about asking them how you can help them. First you help them, then they will help you. You can start by asking someone for help in finding a job, but it's better for you to ask how you can help them first. You never know what they might ask. Maybe they need advice on something. Maybe they want to ask you a question that you can help them with. Then, when you help them with their problem, they might be more inclined to help you with your problem - finding a job."

Carlos said, "That's interesting... that logic doesn't necessarily only apply in finding a job – it could be anything."

Chris responded, "Exactly. I'll give you a couple of examples of two people I went to school with. One person, let's call him Tony, was always one step ahead of the rest of our class at university. He always seemed to have strong relationships with the professors at school. When we graduated from university and started at the accounting firm we worked at, he always seemed to be well-connected with the managers and partners at the firm. He always seemed to be one step ahead of me and the rest of our classmates. Then as we progressed through our careers, when the rest of us were accounting managers he was already a controller. Then, when others in our class were controllers, he was already at a vice president level. He was always one step ahead."

"How did he do that?" asked Ann.

"I would consider him a strong networker," said Chris. "He was always connected with people. He'd help them out first before he needed anything in return. He'd stay after class to ask professors if there was anything he could do at school that could help him improve for the future. When we started working, he'd invite his managers to lunch so he could talk to them about their careers and how they got to where they were. He'd invite people who were senior to him to sporting events so that he could build relationships with them. He was always giving first. When I got into recruitment, Tony was one of the first people to congratulate me on getting into recruiting, wished me luck, and asked if he could take me to lunch to celebrate my new career. He'll still call me once or twice a year to see how things are going with me and always sends me a holiday card each year."

Carlos said, "That's interesting." The others nodded.

Chris continued, "Yes, Tony is great about either offering or doing something for someone before needing something. That's the true art of networking: giving before expecting anything back. Tony taught me about staying in touch with people. With Tony's idea, I developed my own style where I was committed to contacting everyone I knew at least once a year in one form or another, even if it was just to say have a good summer, or Happy New Year, without expecting anything in return. Some people respond, but many don't take the time to initiate a contact themselves or even send a courtesy note back."

Ann said, "I have no time to do that kind of thing."

Chris responded, "You can and should make the time to do it. It will pay off for you in the future in more ways than you think. Do it once a year and you'll find it will definitely pay off for you somewhere, somehow, sometime. Tony taught me that life lesson. Networking is not about asking someone for a job. It's not about asking for something without expecting to give something. *Networking is about building relationships.*"

Ann said, "I always thought networking was about having as many contacts as possible on a list somewhere."

Chris continued, "It's both about quality and quantity. I mentioned I had two examples. Let me tell you about another guy from my class. Let's call him Jerry. Jerry is an extremely bright guy. Jerry received the same educational background as Tony and I; however, Jerry only contacted people when he needed something from them. I would see Jerry at class reunions every few years and sometimes when some common friends got together. When I spoke with him at these events, the conversations would always be about him and his career. It was always about what he was doing and what I could do for him because I was a recruiter. He would only contact me if he needed something. He never asked about what I was doing, my job, my family, or if he could help me with anything. Well, guess what happened? He lost his job that he was at for 10 years and he called me first to ask me to help him find a job. Now, all things being equal, if both Jerry and Tony were looking for a job at the same time, who do you think I would try harder to help?"

Carlos said, "Tony, because he did things for you before you needed something from him."

Chris nodded.

Carlos continued, "You know, I never thought about it that way. A lot of people have helped me in my career and getting the jobs that I had, but I never thought to ask them how I can help them or how I could return the favour. I never even clued in that way."

Chris said, "Over the years I've placed many people in new jobs, many of whom have gone on to do very well with those companies. However, they never touch base with me and they forget about me. I might be able to help them even more – maybe by helping one of their family members get a job or even helping their companies find staff. I send people articles that I think might be of interest to them. Most of the time people don't even thank me for doing that. I do things to help people – some people return the favour at some point; others don't."

Raj asked, "So, all I need to do is offer to help someone and that's networking?"

Chris answered, "Well, to summarize, I guess it's one way to look at it. Networking is about building relationships with people. It's about helping people. It's about getting to know who they are and what makes them tick. It's about helping someone or giving them something without expecting anything in return. Think about my school friend Tony when you think about networking."

Ann smiled, "This is great information."

"There's too much taking in this world and not enough giving," Chris noted. "You have to listen to others and find clues about how you can help them first, before expecting anything in return."

Raj said, "But, Chris, I need to find a job now. This giving thing that you're talking about sounds like it's going to take a lot of time to do, and I can't really wait."

Chris responded, "I understand Raj, but if you have the mindset of wanting to help someone first you'll find that the rewards are going to come faster and greater than if you just ask for help in finding a job right away. First you ask people to talk about themselves – their family, life, work. Then you can ask how you can help them. They might say they don't need help, but the smart people will ask how they can help you. That is your opportunity to let them know of your situation and ask them to help you in your job search. This should be in addition to all the other things that you should do in your job search. Does that make sense?"

Raj nodded, "Yes, very much so. But I assume that not everyone will ask how they can help me, after I ask if I can help them."

"Yes, that is true," responded Chris. "There will be a number who won't ask you. In those cases, I would suggest asking them if they can help you nonetheless."

Carlos commented, "One of the things that I do that works well for me when it comes to networking is that I keep a list of everyone I meet, where I met them, and anything about them I know – for example their likes, hobbies, or anything else that makes them unique. That way it helps me stay organized."

"Great tip!" said Chris.

"Is there anything else you would suggest about networking, Chris?" asked Ann.

Chris replied, "Yes, there is quite a bit. It's getting a little late, but here are three more quick points. One is the hidden job market. Finding a job through the 'hidden job market' can be very powerful."

Raj said, "Yes, I've heard that phrase but not really sure what it means – can we talk about that next week?"

"Absolutely!" said Chris. "The second thing is that I'm going to make you copies of an article that I wrote before you leave tonight on networking tips (*Appendix 4*). This might be able to help you with your networking."

"And the third point?" asked Ann.

"That is, that everyone should be networking!" said Chris. "Networking is just as important for new graduates as it is for experienced professionals. It should be done regardless of whether you're working or not. It's easy to get frustrated trying to network but it's a journey with undefined results!"

"You've been really helpful, Chris," said Ann. "In light of today's meeting, is there anything we can help you with?!"

"Maybe helping me with copying my article?" smiled Chris.

At that point, they wrapped up the meeting for the week and agreed to talk about the hidden job market next week.

CHRIS' THREE POINTERS:

1. Everyone knows people – make a list.

2. Thank everyone you meet.

3. Give before asking for something.

CHAPTER TEN

"HOW CAN I TAP INTO THE HIDDEN JOB MARKET?"

As the four met for the following week's meeting, they were all excited to continue the previous week's discussion about networking. They all sat down and were ready to jump right into discussion.

Chris started, "I know there were a lot of things that we talked about last week, but I want to stress how important networking is in helping you find a job. I wanted to go into some more detail about things that you can do to find a job through networking. But before that, I'd like to share a statistic about networking that has been out there for many years related to finding a job."

Ann asked, "What's that?"

Chris said, "For many years, the conventional thinking has been that most jobs are found through networking. In fact, some statistics indicate that 80-90% of all jobs are never advertised and are filled by networking. This is referred to as the 'hidden job market'. Many times I'll speak with a client about a position they're looking to fill and I might think of one or two strong candidates for the client right away, but I might never advertise the position since I can go directly to the candidates that I think would be good for that position. Many times a company also may not advertise an open position because they hire someone who is referred by one of their employees. Sometimes companies pay their own employees bonuses for any new employees they refer – these are commonly known as 'referral bonuses' and they could be money, time off, or other incentives."

Carlos nodded his head and commented, "Yes, we do that in our company right now. We pay an amount to any existing employee who refers a new employee to our company."

Chris continued, "Many companies do that. Bottom line is that positions are filled the majority of the time through who knows who and not necessarily what someone's qualifications are. I mentioned a couple of weeks ago about how I got a summer job at a bank when I was 16 years old because of who my parents knew. I also mentioned before how clients who are looking to fill a position and have five required skills end up hiring someone who doesn't have all those skills through a referral."

Ann asked, "Chris, how can I tap into this hidden job market?"

Chris began, "Well, Ann, the hidden job market is all around us. You can tap into the hidden job market anywhere at any time. It goes on every day. It's that small business that hires a new administrative assistant who was referred by the accountant's husband. It's that major international communications company who hires their new CEO through a referral from a senior partner at a law firm. It happens at all levels with all companies. How do you tap into that hidden job market? You do so by building your network. I mentioned last week about giving to your network and then you will receive. However, there's also building your network in the first place. Raj, I know you mentioned that you didn't know anyone, but when I started pointing out all the people you knew, you realized that you do know people after all, right?"

Raj nodded his head.

Chris continued, "Well, we all know people. We already know each other. I'm sure if you were to make a list of the people each of us know directly and indirectly, you'd find that our network is huge. All you need to do is find out where the connections are – who knows each other. Doing this does take time. It doesn't happen overnight and it requires patience."

Raj said, "But Chris, I still need to find a job sooner rather than later."

Chris continued, "Bear with me, Raj. The bigger your network becomes, the better the job opportunities you will get. Here are a few things that you can do that will help you in creating and building your network.

First of all, organize your contacts. Build a list of people by name, title, company name, contact information and how you know them. Add notes as necessary. There are many contact management systems available that you can use to manage your list easily or you can just use a basic spreadsheet.

Add your contacts into your system. Don't exclude anyone from your network. Anyone can help you in your job search or in your career. You may be surprised at the list of people you start naming, including relatives or contacts that you already know, people you've gone to school with and people you've met at networking events. Record all the business cards you've ever received. You don't have to be speaking to a president of a multi-national company for you to be able to network with people who can help you. Your list can be as large as you can handle.

Think of how you are going to track your contact with those people. For example, you want to be able to keep track of things such as any referrals to open positions they give you, the names and ages of their kids, or where they like to travel.

As you're adding your contacts, think of how often you want to stay in touch with them. For example, a person who may not be as strong a contact might only be someone you need or want to contact once every three to six months, or even less frequently.

Think about how you're going to build your network. Ask people you meet who they might know and you will be surprised as to how your network can expand from there. Add those contacts to your list also.

Put your networking hat on. As I mentioned last week, you should always be networking, whether you're in job search mode or not. Your network can help you with more than just your job search.

Here are some other ways to network to ultimately tap into the hidden job market:

Join associations
You'd be surprised at how many associations there are out there. Join or volunteer with a local chapter of that association. There are associations and chapters for almost every area of expertise. Do an online search for the associations you're looking for and contact the president to express your interest in getting involved. Typically, volunteers are always needed at association events and this is a great way of networking. Don't be afraid to contact them. If there isn't an association for what you're looking for, start one up and nominate yourself as president of the chapter.

Become your class or work champion
Organize school or work reunions. When you become that class or work champion you are immediately viewed as someone who can connect people. You immediately expand your profile with those people and you can get to know them on a more personal basis.

Network within your community
Try to speak with people who have been in your shoes before. Raj, since you're from India, you should connect with people from India who now live in Canada to see how you can network with them. They will understand

your situation since they have been in your position themselves and can share their ideas of what you can do. Perhaps they have contacts with companies that are within your community.

Network with people similar to you
Find contacts that have similar backgrounds to you. For example, people who went to the same schools as you, people who have taken the same courses or same programs as you. Track people down you used to work with. Find people who you didn't know but have worked at the same company that you have. Make contact with them and add them to your contact list.

Be nice to everyone
Plan to be nice to everyone you meet, not just people you think will be able to help you immediately. You never know who might be able to help you or refer an opportunity to you as you progress through your career.

Always be networking
Don't be one of those who only starts networking when you need something. If you are continuously making contacts, when you begin to look for a change in employment it will come naturally to you and it won't be something you'll need to switch on and off. Your network may pay off even when you're not expecting it in other areas.

Give and you shall receive
If you let others know about job opportunities when *they* might least expect it, they might let you know of opportunities when *you* least expect it. Be sure to pass on anything useful to your contacts when you see something that might interest them.

Do what you say you will
By not doing something that you say you will do, you are sending a message that you're not that reliable. Following up is easy to do. Most of the time it just requires a few minutes of your time and sends a very positive message about you.

Get others talking by asking questions
Don't fall into the trap of thinking that networking is telling others about you. Networking is about giving and sharing information. If you're not comfortable talking, ask questions about the other person - their background, experience(s), what they like doing, etc. so a conversation

will be easier to get started.

It's not just who you know
Your network consists not only those who you know, but also who your contacts know. Keep in mind that if you show that you're willing to pass on names of people you know, others will do the same for you.

Make yourself available
There is never a shortage of places where you can meet people - ask around and you will be amazed at places where people are. Go to networking meetings or volunteer at organizations. Make the time to go to these events, but don't expect a lot the first time you meet someone. Like sales, most of the benefit of networking doesn't come with the first contact.

Thank people for referrals
Be sure to thank people for referrals even if nothing came of them. If something positive happened because of their referral, be sure to let them know. Either way, it will send a positive message that you are thankful for the referral and may encourage them to give you additional referrals.

Tips at networking events
When you go to networking events, keep in mind some simple things:
- Bring business cards
- Listen carefully to what others are saying
- If you're nervous about going to an event alone, ask a friend to join you
- Make eye contact with the person you're speaking with
- Don't keep looking at who is coming into the room every two minutes when you're speaking with someone
- Shake hands and smile with everyone you meet
- Don't talk with your mouth full
- Don't fill up your plate with appetizers at a reception
- Don't just meet one person and talk to that person the whole time… mingle
- Don't flirt
- Don't make offensive jokes

If you follow these suggestions, you will quickly see progress in building your network," smiled Chris.

"There's a lot to remember!" said Ann.

"Yes," commented Chris, "but this is all really great stuff that can be very helpful for each of you in your careers."

Chris continued, "If you only ever stay in your own circle of friends and contacts you'll be limited by the size of your circle. However, by continuously expanding your network you will hear about opportunities that you may never have imagined."

Carlos said, "I've been kind of doing this but didn't realize the potential it had for the future. It makes a lot of sense."

Ann nodded her head. "I've thought about doing this, but never really had time. I've been so into the routine of just waking up each day, going to work, coming home late from work and being just too tired to do anything. Weekends I just want to relax and unwind."

Carlos said, "Ann and Raj, maybe the three of us can do more networking."

"I'm always up for networking – please include me in anything you do!" Chris responded.

Raj said, "This is definitely great information. In fact, I am going to start by contacting someone that I know from my country who lives here now. I didn't think of contacting him before today. I'll be able to start building my network."

Chris said, "I'm glad this discussion is worthwhile to you. Remember, the hidden job market is *extremely* powerful. Even if you think you don't know a lot of people, you might be surprised when you set out to make your list of how many people you really know, and how that group of people can help in finding a new position."

Ann indicated that she needed to leave as she still had some work to do that night, and so the meeting finished.

CHRIS' THREE POINTERS:

1. The hidden job market happens every minute of every day. Join in.

2. Organize your contacts and stay in touch with them regularly, even after you find a position.

3. Be proactive – don't wait for something to come your way.

CHAPTER ELEVEN

"HOW SHOULD I PREPARE FOR AN INTERVIEW?"

The next meeting began with a short discussion about movies, but the conversation quickly turned about opportunities available for Raj.

"So, Raj, you called me on Monday to let me know that you have some opportunities that are happening? I'm glad to hear things are progressing!" said Chris.

"Yes!" smiled Raj. "When we talked about getting experience, you suggested having informational interviews so I was able to line up a few. As a result of an informational interview, I now have a real job interview in a few weeks and I'm very excited. In preparation for this, perhaps we can talk this week about interviews? Anything that you can share with me on what I should do, how to prepare for an interview, how not to be nervous, what to say, what I shouldn't say... that sort of thing."

Ann said, "I agree with Raj. There must be so many things that we're supposed to know about interviews, but no one teaches this stuff in school or when we're growing up as you often just hear from others what to do or not do. However, I don't think those other people really know what they're talking about either. I kind of think of interviews like going to a wedding or a funeral – you're never sure what the protocol is, what to say, what not to say, etc."

Everyone laughed.

Ann smiled, "No, but seriously! It would be good to hear anything you can share about interviews and how they work. For example, is there such thing as a standard interview? You're the expert after all!"

"Ok, well let's get into it as there's a lot to cover," started Chris. "I'm not sure if we can cover interviews all in one meeting, but let's try."

"First of all, interviews can be one of the most intimidating aspects of searching for a job. Unfortunately, the fact is, having great credentials alone are not going to land you a job; having great credentials *and* acing an interview can. There are a lot of tips I can share with you," commented Chris.

"There are really no two interviews that are exactly the same. The dynamics of a job interview are unique, because of the variables of the person conducting the interview and their competence in terms of how to conduct one. There is also the unknown of the person being interviewed and their comfort level in an interview. Similar to the fact that many candidates don't really know how they should conduct themselves during an interview, many interviewers don't prepare for an interview or are inexperienced themselves. Often interviewers are in the same boat as candidates – they haven't been trained to do interviews and just learn as they go along."

"I never thought about that!" said Carlos. "I've had the honour of interviewing people for the companies I've been at, but no one really gave me any training on how to conduct those interviews. So, I kind of came up with my own strategy."

Chris said, "Yes, many interviewers themselves don't know a whole lot about interviews. In fact, some of my clients who are presidents in companies ask me for advice on what questions they should ask job seekers during interviews… and keep in mind, those are the company presidents. Many times there are managers in companies who do the interviews and they don't know what to do or ask either. So, basically, sometimes you've got two people meeting about a job, neither of them having much experience in interviewing. In addition, sometimes the person doing the interviewing, for example an HR person, doesn't really know a lot about the position because he or she is interviewing on behalf of a manager of a department. So, you've sometimes got a mess right from the start. It's no wonder that there's a lot of turnover in companies because the process wasn't well thought out from the beginning."

"Yikes!" said Ann.

"Yikes is right!" continued Chris. "The whole interviewing thing is actually a funny process. It's kind of like trying to find someone to marry and live with just by going on a few dates with them. Sometimes a company settles on a candidate to hire because they don't have any other options and sometimes a person settles on a job because they don't have any other job choices also. Then, when the honeymoon is over, either the company regrets having hired the person because they didn't do their proper screening or the candidate regrets taking the job because they didn't find out enough information before accepting the offer."

"So, regarding the interview," said Chris, "although there is no one way for interviews to go, what I would say is to do your research and prepare for the interview. I would recommend finding out as much as you can prior to the interview. For example, find out about the position, the company, your potential boss, what products the company sells or services they provide, where the company has offices, etc. One of the common questions interviewers will ask is 'What do you know about our company?' If you're going for an interview, you should at least know some things about the company and prepare for that question. I always ask people that question when I interview them for positions with my company. If they haven't even taken the time to research my company it doesn't look good on them. So preparation is the key."

"Do you mean you only need to learn about the company?" asked Ann.

"Not just that, Ann," replied Chris. "As I mentioned, you should know as much as you can. Really research the position. Find out as much as you can about what the company is going to be looking for in a candidate to fill that position. Think of why they would have picked your resume to interview. What did they see in your resume that interested them? Think of why you are a suitable candidate for the position and the company. What value can you bring to the organization? What do you think makes you the best candidate for the position? If you know anyone that works at that company, try to speak with them ahead of time. Any name-dropping can also be helpful to improve your chances at getting the job!"

"What do you mean by that?" asked Raj.

"What I mean," explained Chris, "is that during your interview it would help your chances, for example, if you mention to the interviewer that you spoke to your friend Susan, who is in their Accounting Department, about the position. It would help create a better bond between you and the interviewer. The interviewer can then speak with Susan about you after the interview is done. All I'm saying is that it might not hurt to name drop a little," smiled Chris.

"Unless the position is confidential or something, right?" suggested Carlos.

"Yes, that would be true - good point," answered Chris. "If the position you're applying for is a confidential position – for example, they're replacing someone in the company – you'll definitely hurt your chances by saying you spoke with someone else about the position."

"Well, how would I know if the position is confidential or not?" asked Ann.

Chris said, "Someone will probably tell you in advance – either the recruiter or the company contact will tell you that it's a confidential search. They'll tell you not to say why you're there when you arrive at reception."

"That seems sneaky," noted Raj.

"Yes, it's sometimes a bit of a cat and mouse game when someone is being replaced confidentially," said Chris. "A lot of companies sneak around advertising the position without their company name on the ad and conduct interviews behind the back of the person who is being replaced – sometimes very early in the morning or after hours so that no one gets any clues. It can definitely be uncomfortable for the organization."

"Why would they be replacing someone?" asked Raj.

"Well, most of the time it is due to the person not doing a good job," said Chris. "Perhaps the manager feels that they have to find someone more capable for the job. Sometimes it could be that the person in the job hasn't improved after being advised that they aren't meeting the expectations of the job. For example, they're always showing up late to work but they don't change even after warnings."

"What if the person in the role finds out that they are being replaced? Has that happened?" asked Ann.

Chris replied "Yes, that's happened. It can make for a very uncomfortable situation for the organization, the employee and their manager. It sometimes leads to the employee who is about to be replaced confronting their boss about it and usually ends with either the person quitting or the person being terminated earlier than planned, before a replacement has been selected."

"That would definitely be an uncomfortable situation," suggested Ann.

"Yes," commented Chris, "it can be quite an interesting time. Sometimes it can also get really nasty. It's fairly similar to when someone finds out their spouse was cheating on them… a lot of emotions are involved."

Carlos said, "Wow, I hadn't heard of that kind of thing before! Doesn't sound like it would be a lot of fun… Any other interviewing tips?"

"Absolutely!" answered Chris. "Another tip is to prepare for the kind of interview that will take place, if you can find out ahead of time. For example, is there only going to be one interviewer meeting you? Are you going to be meeting more than one person, either together or separately? What are the names, titles and backgrounds of who you will be meeting?"

"How would I find out this information?" asked Ann.

"Just ask whoever sets up the interview for you, so you can mentally prepare for it," replied Chris. "Sometimes you will be able to find out ahead of time, but not all the time."

The others nodded their understanding.

Chris continued, "The next thing you want to do is prepare for behavioural interview questions."

The others looked puzzled. "Behavioural interview questions? What are those?" asked Ann.

Chris began, "Well, there are the usual standard interview questions, such as:
- Tell me about your strengths.
- Tell me about your weaknesses.
- Tell me about yourself and your experience.
- Why should we hire you for this position?
- What can you bring to/offer our company?
- Why do you think you're the best candidate for this position?
- What do you know about our company/the position?
- Why did you leave your last job?
- Where do you want to be in five years or what are your goals?
- If we call your references, what would they say about you?

Questions like that… pretty typical."

"Some of those are tough questions," said Ann.

"Yes, they are, but those are the standard types of questions that an interviewer will ask you and you should have answers ready for those types of questions," said Chris. "Keep your answers brief. As you're answering, maintain eye contact with the interviewer to make sure they are listening. Watch for non-verbal cues that tell you that they are still listening. For example, if they sit back in their chair or stop taking notes, this may be a sign that they've stopped listening attentively."

"Good points," said Raj.

Chris continued, "Then there are behavioural interview questions that I mentioned. These interview questions uncover what you would do in situations that might be a part of the job for which you are applying. Examples of these could be:

- Describe a situation in which you were able to use persuasion to successfully convince someone to see things your way.
- Describe a time when you were faced with a stressful situation ad what you did.
- Give me a specific example of a time when you used good judgment and logic in solving a problem.
- Give me an example of a time when you set a goal and were able to meet or achieve it."

"Those are *really* tough questions. How do you prepare for those?" asked Raj.

Chris replied, "The best method to prepare for a behavioral interview questions is to start by thinking of three success stories from your past work history. Think of the scenarios and answer the following questions (which are commonly known as the 'STAR' methodology):

- What was the Situation or Task involved? (This is the 'ST' part)
- What was the Action you took? (This is the 'A' part)
- What was the Result? (This is the 'R' part)

These success stories can then be shaped to answer behavioural questions asked during the interview."

"Can you give us an example?" asked Carlos.

"Sure," began Chris, "the company asks you to give an example of a time when you had two deadlines to meet and could only meet one and what did you do. You could reply as follows:

- What was the Situation/Task? – I had two projects that needed to be done and both had to be done by the end of that day but I could only complete one of the two projects. My boss and his boss had each given me a project to complete.
- What was the Action you took? – I called a meeting with both my boss and his boss to determine whose project took priority and which I would do.
- What was the Result? – they agreed as to which project was to be worked on and the other project was given to a co-worker.

Just think it through using that acronym, STAR."

"That doesn't sound too difficult," suggested Ann.

"It's not, but if you're not ready for a behavioural interview question you're going to be caught off guard," said Chris, "so you want to be prepared ahead of time."

"Why do they ask behavioural interview questions?" asked Ann.

Chris replied, "They ask these types of questions to gauge how you handle certain situations. Past behaviour is a good predictor of future behavior: if you did something one way in the past that can be a good predictor of how you'll handle something in the future."

"I see," said Ann.

"Any other types of questions to prepare for?" asked Carlos.

"There are always funny questions that arise," said Chris. "One of my clients who is a controller likes to ask financial analysts he interviews how many gas stations are in the city."

The others laughed. "How can someone *possibly* know that?" asked Raj.

"It's not the answer to the question that actually matters to my client," said Chris. "It's *how* the person replies. He's had people that look at him blankly and say they don't know or they look at him like the guy is stupid and roll their eyes. That tells him a lot about the person. What he's *really* looking for is someone that will at least attempt to logically come up with an answer, whether it's right or not, versus someone who is going to give up even before starting. Remember, he's interviewing for financial analysts so he's looking for someone who is analytical. He's looking for someone that can think for themselves since he needs employees in his office to problem solve and not ask him every time they don't know something. So, an answer that he might be looking for is someone to say 'Although I wouldn't know exactly the answer, I would approximate that there are about three million people who live in the city and there are, let's say, 10,000 people per gas station. So, I would divide 3 million by 10,000 and come up with approximately 300 gas stations in the city'. That would be a smart answer and would be someone that can think on their feet and not give up right away."

"Very interesting!" said Ann. "I suppose a financial analyst should be able to do that kind of math! Anything else to prepare for before an interview?"

Chris answered, "Well, just prepare for different types of interview questions and practice. You have to know what you're going to say. Practice applying your attributes, accomplishments, and success stories to different questions that you might be asked. Focus on how these examples have helped in your previous jobs, therefore demonstrating your value as a potential employee. Practice your answers in front of a mirror, with a friend, or even record a video of your answers and then review. Pay attention to your speech and body language. Are you saying 'um', 'like', or 'you know' a lot, or are you fidgeting? Watching yourself can help you catch and correct these habits and will also help you determine whether your responses sound scripted or natural. Your goal is to sound as natural as possible. Practice, record, and review until your answers sound natural, confident and clear. One more thing - prepare some questions that you'd like to ask the interviewer – questions such as:

- Why is the position open?
- What type of system are you using?
- What are your expectations in the successful candidate?

It's always good to show some interest in the job from the employer's perspective."

"Good to know," said Ann.

Chris pointed out, "I think we've covered a lot about what to do before an interview and it's getting a little late. I do have another handout here which gives you more interviewing tips which should be able to help you (*Appendix 5*)."

Raj, Ann and Carlos thanked Chris for the handout.

"Should we talk about the actual interview itself next week?" asked Chris.

"I think that would be a great idea!" answered Ann.

The four agreed to continue the interview discussion the following week.

CHRIS' THREE POINTERS:

1. Ask to meet people for 'informational interviews'.

2. Prepare thoroughly for interviews such as having strong answers to questions you might be asked.

3. Anticipate and prepare for behavioural interview questions.

CHAPTER TWELVE

"WHAT HAPPENS IN A TYPICAL INTERVIEW?"

Ann, Carlos and Raj were excited to continue hearing about interviews as the three gathered in the boardroom at Chris' office for their weekly meeting. Chris was running a little late as he was finishing up an interview with a candidate. The three were in the middle of talking about the warmer weather as Chris walked in.

Raj couldn't wait to get started and with excitement in his voice, he began. "Chris, I can't wait to hear more about your thoughts on interviews because I'm excited to report that I have an interview this Friday!"

Chris started, "That's great, Raj! Sounds like you have good things happening."

Raj nodded and smiled. "Yes, I have one scheduled in a couple of weeks that I mentioned in our last meeting and then another one this Friday. The position on Friday isn't perfect, and the company is further than I really wanted to commute, but it's certainly a step in the right direction."

Chris added, "That's great, Raj. Yes, we can definitely keep talking about interviews. Before doing that, though, I did want to share an interesting story from this week – it won't take that long."

"I think we're always interested in hearing any stories that you have, Chris," smiled Carlos. The others nodded.

Chris started, "Well, I did a presentation to a group of unemployed individuals this week. People always come up to me after my presentations to ask me questions or make comments, and this time was no different. A woman came up to me, showed me her resume, and asked for feedback on it. I gave her some suggestions on what she could improve on her resume, and I suggested she should send me a copy of it also. She replied to me that she had already sent a copy to 'Derek Michaels'. I told her I didn't know who Derek Michaels was but that she could send me a copy anyway. She told me that Derek was a recruiter from another recruiting firm with whom she had interviewed and that one of her friends had told her that she could only interview/work with one recruiter. As such, she wouldn't be able to send me her resume. I told her that was incorrect and she was free to interview/work with whichever recruiter or recruiters she wanted – she wasn't limited to working with just one recruiter."

"Sounds like maybe she thought it was like working with only one real estate agent when selling a house?" suggested Ann.

"I suppose…" said Chris, "I know in the real estate industry you typically get one broker to list and sell your house, and you sign an agreement with them to be exclusive with them for a certain period. In the recruiting industry you can, and should, work with various recruiters to help you find a job. Although some companies use more than one recruiter to help them fill an open position, recruiters also all have different clients. So, the more recruiters you deal with, the more companies you can possibly touch. I found it surprising about this misconception of the recruiting industry and wonder what other misconceptions might be out there about recruiters."

"Although I knew," began Carlos "that I could deal with multiple recruiters because I have myself in the past, I can see how someone might not know or not know to even ask. If a friend told me that I could only deal with one recruiter I'd probably believe them, but it's probably best to ask a recruiter directly anyway, right?"

"For sure!" said Chris. "You know, I had not heard that comment from anyone before, but I've found over the years that people will say or think many things about recruiters, recruiting firms and staffing agencies. They have misconceptions about how they work, their protocol and how they can help. But it's like anything - if you don't know you should ask, just like the three of you are doing."

"Well, it's not every day that you can speak with a recruiter!" smiled Raj.

"True," said Chris, "but all someone has to do is pick up the phone and call a recruiter and ask them, especially if something doesn't make sense! People are sometimes afraid of asking questions because they think they should know the answer. I remember reading somewhere that kids typically ask a lot of questions, but as they become adults they stop asking questions. I ask people questions all the time – for candidates I ask them what kind of job they are looking for, what salary, what location, etc. For clients I ask them what salary the position pays, what type of person the company is looking for, and so on. You can't get in trouble for asking questions!"

"Thanks for sharing that," said Ann.

"No problem," said Chris. "Ok, let's continue our conversation about interviewing. I know Raj is anxious to talk more about interviews!"

Raj nodded.

Chris said, "Last week we talked about preparing for an interview and the types of interview questions that you might be asked. I also gave you a handout on interviewing tips (*Appendix 5*) last week that perhaps you've had a chance to look at?"

Ann, Carlos and Raj nodded.

Chris asked, "Did you have any specific questions about that?"

Ann asked, "Can you please cover what happens in a typical interview?"

"…and how not to be nervous?" added Raj.

"Oh yes, can't forget about that!" said Ann. "I get really nervous too in interviews. And also, how to not have sweaty hands!"

"How about you Carlos – do you get nervous in interviews?" asked Chris.

Carlos shook his head. "Not really. Sometimes I do, but I always have the attitude that if I don't get the job it wasn't meant to be. It helps me be myself and relax. I also prepare for interviews as much as I can ahead of time. Finding out things like what you talked about last week - the kind of person or people I will be meeting with, the company, the reason for the opening and thinking about what I want to get out of the meeting. I treat interviews as a meeting in which I'm on the same level as the interviewer. I try to understand what they're looking for and how I might be able to fit. I know I'm not going to be a perfect fit for the company for every job, and in reality I'm not going to want every job that I interview for anyway. That helps me relax and stay focused on the discussion. I let things play out naturally, as if I'm speaking with a co-worker. I wasn't always like that and used to get nervous, but as I got older I learned to not be nervous. Of course, I don't get every job I interview for, but experience in having done a few interviews helps."

Chris said, "That is great advice, Carlos. I know interviewing can be stressful for a lot of people. It's natural. The preparation and the expectation of what is going to happen already makes an interview a tense situation. In addition, when you really need a job, for your family or finances, you might panic even more. Most interviewers can pick up signs of nervousness in candidates fairly quickly: quivering of the voice, the cold or sweaty hand when they shake hands with the candidate, the person who talks really fast while answering questions, or the person who says 'you know', 'like', or 'um' too frequently during the interview. Most interviewers will understand nervousness. Don't forget interviewers have been there themselves! Some interviewers actually take pleasure in making job seekers squirm during interviewers."

"You're kidding, right?" said Ann.

"No!" said Chris. "Sometimes they do it to see how the candidate handles pressure situations, especially if the position in question is demanding or has unusual situations."

"Wow!" said Raj. "That's not nice."

"It's reality," said Chris. "An interviewer may think that if you can't handle the pressure of an interview, how will you be able to handle the requirements of a difficult position?"

"Makes sense," said Ann. "Do you have any tips to control nervousness, Chris?"

Chris said, "I would practice an interview with a family member or friends. Put yourself in as real conditions as possible. Get them to ask you questions about your background, your experience, why you think you're a good candidate for the position, etc. Make it as real as possible. Treat it seriously. Think about what you're going to say and rehearse your answers. Display confidence. Practice shaking your friend or family member's hand, looking them in the eyes, smiling and saying 'Nice to meet you', even if it feels awkward. Another helpful trick is to sit with your palms up under the desk. This lowers your blood pressure and air dries your palms. One other thing a recruiter I know advises his candidates going for an interview is to sing a song before going into the interview – that might help also. I'm happy to do a real interview with each of you whenever you'd like."

"That would be excellent!" said Ann.

"I'll be the first to take you up on that, Chris," said Raj.

"No problem!" smiled Chris. "Maybe you can stay after our meeting today and we can do a role play since your interview is coming up?"

"Yes, that would be fantastic – thank you!" said Raj.

"Another point I'd like to talk about is when a recruiting firm contacts you for an interview," continued Chris. "If they do, make sure to go for the interview, even if they don't have a specific position in mind for you, or even if you feel it might be a waste of your time. Every so often I will bring someone in for an interview because I think they have a good background, even though I might not have a specific position for them at the time. I do this because I'd like to meet with them, find out what the person is looking for and then try to 'skill sell' them to companies that might be interested in someone like that."

"What is 'skill selling'?" asked Carlos.

"It's when," began Chris, "a recruiter contacts companies that might be interested in someone with a certain skill or background and asks the organization if they would be interested in that type of candidate. For example, if I interviewed a candidate who is looking for a job that had excellent experience selling widgets, I might call the sales manager at companies that sell widgets to ask if they'd be interested in someone like that."

"Without the candidate knowing?" asked Ann.

"Well, I wouldn't give out the candidate's name when I spoke with that company," said Chris. "I would simply say something along the lines of 'Hello, sales manager at Widget Selling Company. I am a recruiter with Recruiting Firm ABC and I wanted to see if you might be interested in hearing about an excellent sales representative who has a lot of experience selling widgets. Would you like to hear more?' I would then see if I can get my candidate an interview."

"Umm, what's a widget?" asked Raj.

Chris smiled. "A widget is just a fictitious item – it's not real. It's just a pretend small gadget or device. People just refer to widgets to represent a pretend product."

"Does skill selling work a lot?" asked Ann.

"Sometimes," said Chris. "Not all the time, but if I can get a good candidate with a skill set that is hard to find and connect them with a company that could really use someone like that, I might be able to get an interview for that candidate and ultimately make a placement. It can be a win-win-win situation. The client wins because they get a new employee who has specific experience that might be difficult for them to find on their own, the candidate wins because they get a new job, and we win because we get a placement fee. However, none of that happens if a candidate doesn't come in for an interview in the first place. Either way, if you go in for an interview with a recruiter, you never know where it might go from there. Most recruiters have a database where they input information about candidates that have been interviewed and that information can be searched by the recruiter if an appropriate position comes up later. It's a great way for a candidate to get their name out there. However, I've heard so many candidates say to me 'I'll only come to meet with you if you have something specific for me' and don't bother wanting to come in for an interview. Although I try to explain to them the benefits of meeting, sometimes they don't understand their potential loss."

"Overall great tips so far, Chris," said Ann. "Any other tips for interviews?"

Chris replied, "I have lots of tips. Another point to keep in mind is that interviewers can usually tell if you're going to be a fit for the position or for the company in the first few minutes of an interview. After that, most of the time the rest is just 'filler'."

"How do they know so fast?" asked Ann.

"Experienced interviewers have a good idea of who is going to fit into the company's environment," explained Chris. "Without a doubt, a candidate who shows passion, commitment and intelligence has a much better chance of landing a position right from the start. However, think of the companies that you've worked at – you know the kind of people that are there and the types of people that would fit in and wouldn't fit in, right?"

The three nodded their head.

Chris continued, "Well, an interviewer can usually tell fairly quickly whether you're the kind of person and the type of personality that would fit in with their team. That's the one thing that you usually don't know before you go in for an interview - the culture of the group and what kind of people are in there. The interviewer will know that. So you can only do your best, be yourself, and hope that you are the kind of person that fits into their organization."

"That's so true!" said Carlos. "I can tell fairly quickly when I interview someone for my organization whether they'll fit in with our culture and company or not. We have a certain type of person that works in my company."

"Yes, I guess that's true for where I'm at also," said Ann. "There's a definite kind of person that will fit into our company, although it's hard to put a finger on it."

"Here are a few more quick interviewing tips," said Chris. "Try to keep these in mind when you're prepping for an interview.

- Smile when you meet the interviewer and during the interview.
- Shake the interviewer's hands firmly – don't be a 'limp fish' when you shake hands. Also, Ann, if your hands get sweaty have something in your pocket before the interview to dry off your hands.
- Avoid wearing perfume/cologne, don't smoke before your interview, don't chew gum and pop a mint before arriving. Just make sure you finish the mint before your interview starts!
- Be confident.
- Turn off anything that might interrupt the meeting, like a cell phone.
- Make notes during the interview, so bring paper, pen and a portfolio to the interview.
- Bring a list of references in case you are asked for them.
- Take your time answering questions and be as honest as you can.
- Speak clearly and don't ramble – answer the questions concisely.
- Don't talk badly about previous bosses or companies that you worked at.

Also, have some questions ready to ask as there will probably be an opportunity to do so at some point during the interview.

Questions you *can* ask the interviewer:
- Is this a new position? If not, why is this position open?
- Can you please describe the ideal candidate you are looking for?
- How do you feel my qualifications compare to your expectations for the role?
- What are the next steps in the interview process?
- When will you be making a hiring decision?
- What opportunities are there for advancement?
- Who would I be reporting to?
- What are the hours expected for this position?
- What are some of the short term objectives of this position?
- What are some of the long term objectives of this position?
- Who does this position report to?
- What advancement opportunities are available for the successful applicant?
- Do you see any significant company changes in the near future?
- How is the successful candidate evaluated for this position?
- What accounts for success in the company?

Questions *not* to ask the interviewer:
- What does your company do? (Do your research ahead of time!)
- If I get the job when can I take time off for vacation? (Wait until you get the offer to ask about benefits.)
- Can I change my start and end time if I get the job? (If you need to figure out the logistics of getting to and from work don't mention it now.)
- Did I get the job? (Don't be impatient. They'll let you know.)
- What are the benefits? (This can be discussed when an offer is made.)
- How much is the position paying? (This can be discussed when an offer is made. Don't talk about salary, especially in a first interview, unless the interviewer brings it up!)

A few ideas that I'm sure you will find helpful in preparing for interviews..." smiled Chris.

"I know it's getting late, Chris, but do you have any other funny stories about interviews?" asked Carlos.

"Well, there are really so many to share!" smiled Chris. "There are a lot that really make me wonder. For example, the candidate who thought it was okay to bring her kids to an interview. I mean, sometimes I realize it can't be helped, but candidates should really make an effort to not bring their kids with them to interviews or ask permission from the recruiter beforehand if necessary and explain the reason(s). Then there was the candidate who brought his wife to a final interview, because he couldn't make a decision about whether to accept the position or not, and wanted her opinion. Then there was the candidate who took a phone call during the actual interview."

"Are you kidding?" asked Ann.

"I'm not kidding!" said Chris. "Oh yes, and there was another time when I came into an interview room and the candidate I was going to interview was on his cell phone. Instead of hanging up quickly, he stuck out his index finger to me, covered the cell phone and asked me to come back in five minutes so he could finish his call."

The four broke out into laughter.

Chris continued, "Just be prepared for anything when you go or an interview. I've heard interviewers ask people some unusual questions in interviews, such as:

- Are you nervous?
- What's the worst mistake you ever made at a previous job?
- Sell this pen to me in five minutes.
- If you could be any animal, what would it be and why?
- If you were a product, how would you go about improving yourself to be more sellable?

Bottom line is to prepare for and plan for *anything*!" said Chris. "For every different type of interviewer there are different styles that each might use. Ann, when you asked me earlier what happens in a typical interview, the reality is that no two interviews are ever the same. Some interviews could be as short as five minutes, others could be as long as three hours or more. It depends on the people involved, the role, and the time available, how much of a fit the candidate is to a particular position, etc."

Ann nodded.

Chris continued, "After the interview, write down as much as you can remember, the names of people you met with, your impressions, both positive and negative, and any other information you might find useful later. It will help you remember details of the interview if you get a second interview."

"How many interviews are there usually?" asked Raj.

"Well," began Chris, "I've seen as few as one and as many as 10 to 12 interviews for the most senior positions."

"That many?" asked Ann.

"Yes, depending on the seniority of a position before an offer is made," said Chris.

"I can't imagine going back and forth to a company 10 to 12 times and not knowing if I'm going to get the position. Wow!" said Ann. "What's the average?"

"Usually two to three interviews is the average," said Chris. "The first interview is just a general interview that the organization has with all selected candidates while the second interview is usually more detailed. During the second interview, you might meet some of the other members of the team. The third interview usually includes a job offer. But each interview process is different. Companies might have six to ten candidates in the first round of interviews, then bring back two to three candidates for the second and third round of interviews and make an offer to one of those candidates in the fourth interview."

"Interesting information," said Ann.

"Today was excellent!" smiled Raj. "I'm much more prepared for my interview Friday."

"Glad to hear that!" said Chris.

The four agreed that they had made good progress, agreed to wrap up their meeting and meet up again the following Wednesday at the same time. Ann and Carlos wished Raj good luck on his interview. Chris and Raj stayed after the meeting to do a mock interview.

CHRIS' THREE POINTERS:

1.   Use multiple recruiters to help you in your search – don't rely on just one.

2.   Control nervousness for an interview by being prepared.

3.   Have questions ready to ask the interviewer.

CHAPTER THIRTEEN

"WHAT DO I PUT IN MY COVER LETTER AND THANK YOU LETTER??"

As Chris met with Ann, Raj and Carlos for their weekly meeting, everyone was curious to find out how Raj's interview from the week before had gone.

Raj explained, "Well, it was not as good as I had hoped. The interview lasted about 10 minutes and the HR person only asked me a few basic questions and finished up the interview fairly quickly. I was very disappointed after the interview. I came home to my wife and told her what had happened and we were both sad. I couldn't believe that it was so short. After all the preparation I had done and our role play from last week, I don't get it. I did everything that you had suggested over the last two weeks, Chris."

"I understand, Raj," said Chris. "I think it depends on the interviewer and the position that you were being interviewed for. It may have been that the interviewer felt in the first few minutes that you weren't going to be the right candidate for the role and just didn't want to go further. I don't know, it's hard to say as I wasn't there. I have seen 10 minute initial interviews go nowhere but other times I've also seen the candidate get asked back for another interview, but I don't want to get your hopes up either. You had said that it wasn't the right type of position for you last week, so maybe it's a positive thing. If anything, you had a chance to practice your interview skills."

"It was still upsetting…" said Raj, "but on the positive side, I do have another interview next week, so hopefully that one will be better."

"It doesn't sound like you had a good experience, but maybe next week's interview will be better!" said Ann.

"It's okay, Ann," said Raj. "I guess it was a learning experience."

"What should we talk about this week?" asked Chris.

"It's my turn to make a request, if that's okay, Chris?" Carlos asked. Chris nodded. "I'd like you to discuss cover letters and thank you letters Chris. First of all, I'm not exactly sure when to use them and what I should include in them."

Raj added, "Hmm… I never thought about that. Should I send the person

I met last week a thank you letter? What should I say?"

"All good questions," said Chris. "Let's talk about cover letters first. Cover letters should be one page in length and accompany a resume. They are a good way to address anything related specifically to the requirements of the position that you're applying to, which may not be addressed in your resume. You can highlight things like how you worked on a project that was related to one of the specific requirements of the posting, or that you have similar industry experience. The cover letter is important for several reasons:

- It explains to the recruiter that you are interested in the advertised position. It also details how you became aware of the opening.
- The cover letter is your first opportunity to sell yourself. It is your first introduction into the organization and can get the prospective employer's attention.
- The cover letter allows you to detail how your skills and experiences specifically match the requirements outlined in the job advertisement.
- Managers who conduct hiring for their company find it courteous that you took the time to create a cover letter specific to the requirements of the position.

A personalized, targeted and well-written cover letter is your chance to set yourself apart and pique the employer's interest. Let me go make some copies that may be helpful."

Chris got up and walked away and the group stretched, talking amongst themselves about all that they were learning.

After a few minutes Chris returned. "Here's a checklist of what you should include in your cover letter (*Appendix 6*), copies of a cover letter template (*Appendix 7*) and a sample cover letter (*Appendix 8*)."

"How much do recruiters look at cover letters?" asked Ann.

"Truthfully," Chris started, "and I know this may seem strange, but recruiters who get a lot of resumes, like me, don't typically spend very much time, if at all, looking at cover letters. I typically spend less than a few seconds looking at a cover letter, just briefly glancing at format primarily. With resumes, over the years I've learned to skim through them and this typically gives me enough information for what I need. So I don't usually need to look at a cover letter."

"Why bother to do a cover letter then?" asked Raj.

"Not everyone is an experienced recruiter like me who sees so many resumes," explained Chris. "Plus, don't forget all the benefits I mentioned earlier. You never know who is going to be looking at your resume so it's definitely something you should prepare. But if you were sending your resume to a recruiter who gets piles on their desk, chances are they won't be looking at your cover letter very much."

"What kind of things do you skim for in a resume?" asked Carlos.

"Of course I'm looking for experience, but I also skim for things like grammar, punctuation, format and spelling," explained Chris. "These tell me a lot about how detailed the candidate is and indicates if communication might be an issue. Over the years I've learned to pick up spelling mistakes quite quickly by skimming through resumes. As soon as I see a typo, that person's resume loses credibility for me."

"Do you throw it out if you see a spelling mistake?" asked Ann.

"No," replied Chris, "but it does give me reason for concern. One spelling mistake is really not very good – more than one spelling mistake is very poor. In saying that, it is pretty bad if someone has a spelling mistake on their cover letter or resume, especially with the ability to automatically check spelling so easily now. Poor grammar might indicate to me that English might not be the person's first language. In which case, I might be dealing with a communication issue."

"With people from overseas like me, would you reject my resume if you saw a grammatical error?" asked Raj.

"No Raj," said Chris, "but it would make me more cautious. Everyone should be extra careful of spelling, formatting and grammatical mistakes on their resume. Anyone looking for a job should have someone else proofread their cover letters and resumes to catch grammatical and spelling errors. It should be done by someone you respect who has the confidence to tell you that something is wrong, without you getting defensive about any suggestions they make. It's ironic when someone close to us, like a spouse, suggests you change something we tend not to listen, but when a perfect stranger tells you to change the same thing, we listen."

The others nodded and smiled.

Chris continued, "I may skim through cover letters for more information if someone indicates they are bilingual or they have a certain skill set or have experience within a specific industry that might be relevant for a position I'm trying to fill."

"Wouldn't that be on the resume anyway?" asked Carlos.

"It would," Chris said, "but sometimes people bury something relevant to a position that I'm recruiting for or not include it, without realizing it. For example, they might not have indicated that they're bilingual or it might be in the 'other' section of their resume, so it's not as visible. They might indicate the companies they worked for, but it's not obvious that one of those companies is in the same industry as my client. For example, a recruiter wouldn't necessarily know that the person who worked at XYZ Company was actually in the real estate industry, which is the industry that my client is in. Know what I mean?"

"Yes," said Carlos.

"Any more questions regarding cover letters?" asked Chris.

Everyone shook their head.

"I think the handouts that you gave us will help," said Carlos.

"Yes, they will," said Chris. "Ok, well then let's move on to talk about thank you letters. Thank you letters should be sent out after every interview or every meeting you go to when you're in job search mode. Most recruiters and hiring managers will have a higher opinion of someone who follows up with a thank you letter after an interview."

"What are the benefits of sending out a thank you letter?" asked Carlos.

"A thank you letter shows a potential employer that you are interested in the position, can reinforce some points that you made during the interview, or bring up some points that you forgot to mention. Thank you letters can definitely help increase your chances of getting hired. It demonstrates that you are an organized person and that you have good manners. It can also show the interviewer that you are professional," said Chris. "I would try to get the thank you letter to the person within one or two business days after the interview, otherwise the recruiter might think it was an after-thought. As such, you should send a thank you letter to the person you met last week as soon as possible Raj."

"I'll do that when I get home tonight, Chris," said Raj.

"Should a thank you letter be handwritten, typed, mailed or e-mailed?" asked Ann.

"It really can be any of those," explained Chris. "I find that handwritten letters are generally more memorable, since I get so many emails during the day. However, with email being so fast, that will work also. I actually had one candidate I interviewed who wrote a thank you card and left it with our receptionist right after we finished our interview. It's interesting how I haven't forgotten about that thank you letter all these years!"

"That's funny!" said Carlos.

"In addition," continued Chris, "a lot of people don't ever follow-up again after an interview. However, if a week or two goes by after the interview, you haven't heard back from the employer and you've sent your thank you letter, you should follow-up again to find out the status of the position. If they tell you they selected another candidate for the position, you should ask them for feedback. You could ask them questions such as what you could have improved upon, what you did well, what was the reason(s) the other candidate was chosen, etc."

"If I've followed up after an interview and left a voice mail, but I still didn't get a response from the employer," said Ann, "what do I do then?"

"Well, I would just leave it then," said Chris. "If you've been there for the interview, you've sent a thank you letter, and then followed up by phone or email after that and the interviewer still hasn't got back to you, you can probably assume you didn't get the position. It's unfortunate that you might not get a response, but that happens quite a bit. I think it's because interviewers don't like giving people bad news, so they do nothing. Either that or they're too busy, which I don't really believe. Recruiters should know that it's quite the opposite – most people who didn't get a position want to hear the news first hand instead of not hearing any news. They want to be able to improve for their next interview."

"Exactly," said Ann.

"By the way," continued Chris, "it happened to me years ago before I was in the recruiting industry. I thought I had an excellent interview with a recruiter from a large company. I sent her a thank you letter and followed up a few times leaving messages each time, but she never got back to me. I thought it was quite rude of her. It gave me a bad impression of the company and I figured I wouldn't want to work for that kind of company anyway, so I guess it worked out in the end! I ended up vowing to myself that when I got into recruiting, I would let people know if they didn't get a job (for example, if they followed up with me in the first place)."

"That's really good that you do that…" said Carlos.

"I try," said Chris, "it's tough in the recruiting business because there are so many things that come at recruiters all the time and it gets hard to manage. I could be working at my desk 24 hours a day, seven days a week, answering emails, phoning people, reading every cover letter and resume that comes across my desk, and still not have enough time to do everything. There's only so much one person can do. I've seen a lot of recruiters over the years that aren't organized. They don't call people back or don't really care about their reputation. I think recruiting is a great industry. However, there are a few bad recruiters, like every profession, who give the overall industry a bad name."

"You're right about that," said Ann. "Do you have any sample thank you letters, Chris?"

"Yes, I was thinking you might ask about that so I grabbed some copies of additional thank you letter tips (*Appendix 9*) and a sample thank you letter (*Appendix 10*)," said Chris.

"That's great, thanks," said Carlos.

"You've been so helpful," said Raj.

"I just like trying to help," said Chris.

"Any other questions regarding thank you letters, or anything else that you can think of about cover letters?" asked Chris.

There was silence.

"I'll take that as a no then!" said Chris. "Should we wrap things up for this week?"

Ann, Raj and Carlos nodded their head.

The weekly meeting wrapped up with the four agreeing to meet again the following Wednesday.

CHRIS' THREE POINTERS:

1. Keep your cover letters and thank you letters simple, but make sure to do them.

2. Follow-up with a company if you haven't heard back from them after your interview, and after you've sent your thank you letter.

3. Make sure there are no spelling, grammatical or formatting errors anywhere on your cover letter, thank you letter or resume.

CHAPTER FOURTEEN

"WHAT REFERENCES SHOULD I GIVE?"

The four arrived for the weekly meeting and Chris started by asking what topic was on their minds.

Raj asked, "Well, as you know Chris, I'm new to Canada. No one can give me a reference from work I've done here. Is that going to be a problem?"

Ann noted, "Yes Chris, we haven't talked about references yet, but I've been with my current company for several years now. I wouldn't want anyone calling my current manager and the references from my old positions are somewhat outdated now, so what references should I give?"

Carlos commented, "I always wondered about the whole reference checking process – how it works, who does them, when they're done, can it make the difference between getting a job or not – things like that."

Chris started, "I'm certainly happy to cover those questions. There's a lot to cover with references, so let's get started. References are people that potential employers can contact to find out information about you, your work and your work history. References are typically done by an employer who is considering hiring someone. Most of the time employers do the reference checks close to the time that they're about to make someone an offer for a job. It's not always the best time to do a reference check, but that's usually when it happens."

Raj asked, "Why does it happen when they're about to make an offer?"

Chris answered, "It might be because they don't think about doing the reference checks until after all the interviews are done or they're not sure about asking for references up-front. Either way, most of the time employers do them at the very end of the interview process. I usually like to do the reference checks as early as possible in the process, even before sending a candidate out to an interview with a client if possible, so that I can find out any red flags early. I have found out so much information about candidates through checking their references. I don't like finding something out about a candidate at the very end of a long interview process and then potentially losing a placement because I didn't do a reference check early. It doesn't look good for me or for the candidate."

"Good point," noted Carlos. The others nodded.

Tales from the Recruiter

"So, to continue," said Chris, "reference checks are designed to gather as much information as possible about a candidate from people who can provide information regarding their previous work experience and what they're like. References are given by the person who is applying for the position to the potential employer or to the recruiter. Your references should be people that you've directly reported to or can talk candidly about your work experience, including clients, if you had some. Usually you should have two to three references to give to the employer or the recruiter. It's a good idea to confirm with the references that they are in agreement with you providing their contact information. If a potential employer has said that they're going to contact your references, you should remind your references again to make sure they'll be available. If they are on holidays, let the employer or recruiter know, so that they will have an idea of when they can get hold of your references. That's also another reason why I like to do the references early. If I can't get hold of a reference at the end of the interview process with my client, it might delay my candidate getting a job which could risk me losing my placement."

"What questions are references asked?" asked Ann.

Chris replied, "There are quite a few. Here are some standard basic reference check questions that most recruiters will use:

- Can you confirm the candidate's title?
- Can you describe the candidate's responsibilities in their role?
- What dates did the candidate work for you?
- Did they report to you or to someone else?
- What was their salary? Any bonuses? Benefits?
- What are their strengths?
- What are their weaknesses?
- How were their written and oral communication skills?
- What was their reason(s) for leaving?
- Did they give appropriate notice when they left?
- Would you rehire them again in a similar position?

I will also sometimes ask additional questions depending on the candidate and the type of job that they're applying for."

"Can the answers to these questions actually make someone lose a job?" asked Ann.
"Yes, they can!" said Chris. "There are many employers that will take an

offer away if they find out differences between what the reference said and what the candidate prioritized. Employers have sometimes not gone ahead and offered a position to a candidate even though they were great, because of something wrong with the candidate's references."

"Are they allowed to do that?" asked Raj.

"Well, employers have a right to decide who they want working with them," Chris said. "If a candidate lies about what their title was, their work experience or how much they were earning in a previous position, it puts into doubt the credibility of that candidate. If an employer can't have enough faith to be able to believe that an employee will tell them the truth right up-front, how can they trust that the candidate will be honest when they actually start to work there? In a worst-case scenario, I've seen it where an employer has offered someone a job, the person actually started working at the company, the employer finds out something significantly wrong in a reference, and terminates the employee. So just be careful about what reference names you give to employers. Make sure they will give you a good reference and that your resume is accurate. It goes without saying, but do a good job everywhere you work so that one day a reference won't come back to hurt you. On most occasions a company will offer the position to a candidate 'subject to two or three satisfactory references'."

"What else can you suggest regarding references?" asked Raj.

Chris continued, "Well, before you even get to that, don't lie about dates or your titles on your resume. Leave on good terms with your previous managers and give the appropriate amount of notice. I've seen too many people leave a job without giving a proper amount of notice and their boss keeps that in the back of their mind. Then one day in the future that old boss becomes a reference check. The former boss mentions the bad experience and it reflects poorly on that candidate. Don't be that person who gives two weeks' notice on the first day of their boss' two week vacation, and then the boss has to cut his or her vacation short because they need to find your replacement. They'll remember that and it might haunt you one day. Or don't be that person who puts on their resume that they were at a job for three months but were really only there for a few days and stretched the dates out."

"That's happened?" asked Carlos.

"Yes," continued Chris, "I interviewed a candidate who said she was working at a company for three months and that it was a contract. She told me that she stopped working there because the contract finished. I asked her for a reference from that company but she made up an excuse that the company doesn't give references. So, I called them anyway and asked to speak to the manager there. The contact was happy to tell me how awful the candidate was and not to hire her. He told me all about how she had worked there for all of two days then told him that she had an illness and then disappeared. She never provided a doctor's note to him. He then told me that she called him about six weeks later and said that she had recovered and was able to start working again. He reluctantly agreed to have her come back the following Monday and then she didn't even show up or call. He never heard anything from her again. He was surprised that she had given his name as a reference. I told him that she hadn't – that she had told me that their company didn't provide references but I called anyway. He couldn't stop laughing when I told him."

"Wasn't the reference concerned that he was saying something that could get them in trouble?" asked Carlos. "For example, that he was saying bad things about this employee and if the candidate didn't get the job that the candidate might sue him or his company?"

Chris replied, "Yes, that certainly could be a possibility, but I would think the chances of that happening are fairly minimal. I haven't heard of that happening, although I'm sure it does. References do need to be careful about what they say."

"Are you allowed to call a reference if the candidate doesn't give you a name at a company?" asked Carlos.

"Yes," replied Chris, "when a candidate comes in for an interview they fill out and sign our application form saying that we can 'perform reference checks or other background checks as required'. That basically gives us the right to check a person's background. A lot of times a candidate won't even know all the people we contact to check on references. That's why it's good to be nice to everyone you work with!"

"How much notice should you give when leaving a job?" asked Ann.

Chris said, "Ann, that's a great question. Generally, two weeks' notice is appropriate. However, if you're at a senior level and it's going to take your employer more time to find your replacement or cross-train a new person, three or four weeks' notice might be appropriate. Some people at very senior levels, such as CEOs of major corporations, may give six months to a year notice if necessary. If you're on a contract and you've made a commitment to stay for a certain period because you're on a major project, such as a system implementation, you should commit to that contract for the entire duration."

Carlos said, "Yes, I had a person leave during the middle of a large IT project in our company without giving a lot of notice because she found a full-time job, and we weren't impressed with her. She's going to regret that she did that one day as it's going to come back to haunt her in a reference check."

"Yes, that does happen," agreed Chris. "What goes around comes around... you know what they say about karma..."

The others smiled.

"I wanted to cover off a couple of the questions that you had asked me earlier," continued Chris. "First, Raj asked about being new to Canada and not having references. That is a tough issue, Raj, because unfortunately there are recruiters who may discredit your references from overseas in India. They are an unknown reference. The foreign reference may have nothing to lose by giving you a good reference. It may also be hard for a recruiter to determine the reliability of your references. As well, with the time difference in India there it might be difficult to get in touch with your references, so recruiters might not even try. Finally, your work experience might not be as relevant here as it might be there. My suggestion would be to have your list of references available when you go to interviews and offer them to the employer. There will be some employers who will do the references and others who won't. Try to start building a list of references within Canada, even if they are not work-related. For example, if you volunteer for a not for profit organization, add anyone there that might provide a reference."

Raj nodded his head in agreement.

Chris continued, "Ann, earlier you mentioned you didn't want an employer contacting your current employer since you've been at your company for several years. You should try to contact people that you worked for previous to this position that you still stay in touch with and provide those references. Perhaps you could also provide co-workers that you trust that you're currently working with or have worked with recently who have left the company. If you have any external clients, suppliers or vendors they might be able to confidentially act as a reference. Most employers will understand that you can't provide your current manager's name as a reference, regardless of how long you've been there. They will know that you don't want them finding out that you're looking for a position until you're going to resign. It's a little under-handed trying to provide references while you're working, and people don't like doing it. But sometimes, you need to do that when you're looking for a job."

"I understand.," said Ann. "Any other suggestions you have about reference checks?"

Chris replied, "Yes, here are a few more:

- Have your reference list ready so that you can give them to an employer at a first interview – A candidate who comes prepared with references in the first interview will impress the interviewer.
- The reference list should be neatly typed on one page with your name at the top and the relationship that you had with each of the references.
- Use only work-related references, unless you don't have any work experience like a student. In that case, you could use teachers/professors or people that know you well.
- Stay in touch with your references – keep them informed of your employment status.
- Don't give friends as references – employers will generally discount those types of references since they probably wouldn't be objective.

Again, I trust these will be helpful," remarked Chris.

The three nodded.

As they wrapped up the meeting, Raj quickly skimmed through his notes from that day's meeting on references. He sighed and said "So much to remember…" as his voice trailed off.

With that, the four wrapped up their meeting for the week.

CHRIS' THREE POINTERS:

1. Make sure to have a sheet with your references listed when you go for an interview and give it to the interviewer even if they don't ask.

2. Give your references some advance warning when someone may be calling them on a reference.

3. People who you reported to are better references to give than co-workers.

CHAPTER FIFTEEN
"IS THERE A PERFECT JOB?"

Chris was excited to have the next weekly meeting with Ann, Raj and Carlos because he had a story to share. Chris always liked telling stories – whether they were stories about candidates, clients, or both.

"Welcome to the weekly meeting," Chris began. "I have a story for you, following up on our meeting last week regarding references. I had a woman apply for a sales position that I have with our company and I brought her in for an interview to my office last Thursday. She was working for a company that I used to work at but I never knew her before our interview. I did know her manager since I had worked with him, although she asked me not to call him as a reference check because she didn't want him to know that she was looking for a position. I respected her wish. I met her at two o'clock and she said she could meet because she was expected to be out on the road at sales calls, so it wouldn't be unusual that she was out of the office at that time. She seemed to be a very good candidate. After our interview, I wanted to speak with her again on the phone so I asked her to call me at four o'clock Friday afternoon. She called me precisely at four o'clock as agreed and we continued our discussions about our company and what she was looking for. For some reason, I had a funny feeling that something wasn't right about her, but I didn't know exactly what it was. I reviewed my interview notes and when I had asked her about how much notice she would need to give to her current employer she told me one week."

"One week is short, right Chris?" asked Ann. "You said last week we should give two weeks' notice."

"Yes Ann," said Chris, "especially since I've worked for the same company, and two weeks is definitely the norm there. I would have expected her to know that given that she's in the recruiting industry. I know there are companies that walk you to the door when you resign because they don't want you hanging around the office if you're leaving, especially if you're in a sales position. Many employers don't like sales people calling their clients and telling them that they're leaving. They'd rather the person left as soon as they give their notice. So this one week notice was a red flag for me. I also reviewed my notes as to her reasons why she was leaving the company. She said that she wasn't happy there, although she was only there for about a year and a half. So I called her workplace, blocking my phone number and asked for her. Guess what happened?"

Raj said, "She didn't work there anymore?"

"Exactly!" said Chris. "They told me she hadn't worked there for about two months."

"So, what did you do?" asked Raj.

Chris started, "Well, last weekend I called her again and asked her to reconfirm that she was still working there. For some reason her story now changed. She told me that she had given her notice. So, now she was just digging an even deeper hole for herself. She had never mentioned anything about giving notice when I spoke with her on Thursday or Friday. So I asked her why she would give notice without another position in hand. I wanted to see how far she would go with her lies. She answered that she was confident she could find another job quite quickly and restated that she wasn't happy there. So I asked her if I could then speak with her boss on a reference check since I knew her boss. There was nothing for her to lose especially since she had already supposedly given notice. Her story was starting to unravel."

"So, what did she do?" asked Carlos.

"Well, there was a brief pause on the line, and then she hung up on me!" replied Chris.

"What?!" said Ann.

"She hung up on me!" repeated Chris. "She got caught. I was going to call her back and say something like 'I think our connection got lost' but I didn't want to push it. She got caught and she didn't know what to do. That's the reason you need to be 100% honest about your experience and your situation when you're going for interviews because I probably would have hired her had she not lied. She had nothing to lose by telling me she wasn't working there anymore. I found out later through some old co-workers that she was fired from her job for regularly being late for work!"

"Wow…" commented Ann.

"Wow is right. Just be careful, is all I can say. I'm not sure why people lie about that kind of stuff, but recruiters who have been around for a while, like me, know a few of the tricks people use. I've seen so many things…" said Chris.

"I didn't know people were like that!" said Ann.

Chris responded, "Yes, they can be." There was a brief pause and Chris continued "So, what should we talk about today?"

Carlos started, "As you know, Chris, I've had some good luck with opportunities and positions I've worked at so far in my career. I'm curious about your thoughts on this – is there such a thing as a perfect job?"

"That's an interesting question," said Chris. "I guess it really depends on what you like to do and who you are. I think I'm in my perfect job. I truly love everything I do. I enjoy the people I work with and I enjoy dealing with my clients. There's not a day that I come to work and I'm not completely enthused with what I do. So, for me, the answer is yes. I have found the perfect job for me. I enjoy working long hours on what I do and it doesn't really feel like work. I think that's ultimately the true definition of a perfect job – you love what you do. If you enjoy doing your favourite thing - whether it's going to a sports event, out for dinner, etc. - as much as you enjoy working at your job, you've probably found perfection. I'm there right now. I'm not saying it will be like that forever, but at this time in my life, I'm there."

"That's incredible," said Raj.

"True," said Chris, "but that's just me and it took me a long time to get there. I hunted this job out. I made a list of everything I wanted in my job and went after it."

"What was on your list?" asked Ann.

Chris replied, "I put everything I could think of on my list, including how I wanted to dress, what type of work I would be doing, who I would be dealing with, what hours I wanted to work, etc. My list had over 50 points on it. I made the list before I even knew what job I was going to get. It took me some time to make that list and I did it over a few weeks so that I made sure to capture all the points I wanted. Once I had my list I started matching it up with every job description I could find. I also looked at the North American Industry Classification System (NAICS) Codes. These are similar to the Standard Industrial Classification, or SIC (pronounced 'sick') codes. I reviewed them to see what industries appealed to me. I had a completely open mind when I was doing that."

Tales from the Recruiter

"What are the NAICS or SIC codes?" asked Ann.

"They are a list of every industry," said Chris. "At a high level, they show agriculture, mining, construction, manufacturing, banking, retail trade, etc. industries. At a detailed level, they include warehouse storage, masonry contractors, etc.," said Chris.

Ann nodded.

Chris continued, "Ultimately, it took a long time to come up with the perfect match. Without making my list first I would have just been drifting along considering any opportunity that came to me, instead of me going out and finding that opportunity."

"Sounds like a lot of work," said Carlos.

"Yes, no doubt it is," agreed Chris. "I think generally most people apply for a position that they see advertised or someone tells them about an opportunity. If they get offered the job their choice then becomes taking the new job or staying where they are. They're not really managing or taking control of their career by doing that. They're being reactive as opposed to being proactive. The best thing I would suggest to do is write up a list of everything you want in a perfect job. For example, your list could include which system you'd be using, or the type of manager you'd like to work for, or even a place that has a refrigerator so you can bring your lunch. It doesn't matter what's on your list, since it's yours. Money doesn't have to be on your list although that will help if it can define your perfect job. If you love what you do, and you've found your perfect job, the money will come one way or another. Even more important, money will be secondary since you'll love what you do. As I mentioned a few weeks ago, I've met many people over the years that make tremendous amounts of money in their jobs or careers but they truly hate what they're doing. They're in their current job or career because of the money, but they're unhappy in their lives. Their family lives suffer as a result. They're going to a job every day just going through the motions. They get there at nine o'clock in the morning and can't wait for the clock to strike five o'clock in the afternoon. In some survey results I've read up to 80% of people hate their jobs. That's a lot of people who are unhappy in their lives. Do something that you love and you're on your way to having that perfect job. Find that perfect job and it will be something that you love to do. Work won't seem like a chore if you can find that. You will be enthused about everything you do if you find that. You'll work long hours because it doesn't feel like work."

Chris was getting more excited and he was talking much faster. He was out of breath.

The others sat silent. There was a pause in the room. No one knew what to say. Neither Ann, Raj or Carlos had ever thought of making up a list of what they wanted in their jobs or careers. The thought had never crossed their minds. This was quite a revelation. Neither Carlos nor Ann was currently in their perfect job.

Chris continued, "Most people will have a general idea about what they want to do such as acting, accounting, IT, sales, customer service, etc. The choices are endless. But there's more. Where? How? When? Who? Which? What size of company? How much vacation? What do you want to wear to work? What hours are you looking to work? Work from home, on the road, or at an office? Or a combination? The list of questions goes on and on. The answers to all those questions will give you the framework for your perfect job. You need to be realistic, of course. If you're not an athlete, you might not be cut out to play with the New York Yankees!"

The others smiled.

Chris continued, "Once you have your list, show it to anyone you think will help you find that perfect job, and tell them those job characteristics will make that happen for you. Some may laugh at what's on your list. Ignore them – it's your list and the points are what things are important to *you*. The next thing to do, once you figure out what the perfect job is, is to go after it. Where can you find that job? Which companies hire people for those positions? What do you need to do to get that job? Keep in mind that getting that perfect job may not happen overnight – it might take months or even years to get there – but now is your chance to plan your career and go after your perfect job!"

"How do you go after it?" asked Carlos.

"Call people who are in that industry or role. Pick up the phone and call them," said Chris. "Share with them that you're looking for what they're doing. Ask to meet with them so that you can find out more. Tell them that they're in the perfect job that you're looking for!"

"They'll just laugh and won't give you the time, won't they?" said Ann.

Chris replied, "No way. Let me put it in a different way, Ann. Say someone called you at your work tomorrow. They said that they had done a lot of thinking about their career and thought that you were in their perfect job. They told you that they wanted to be working in a similar role to yours, and wanted to meet with you to talk about how you might be able to help them get that perfect job. Wouldn't you at least spare a few minutes to talk to them?"

Ann said, "I'd probably laugh and think they were crazy. Why would they want my kind of job?"

Chris said, "Who knows, but if they sounded passionate over the phone and kept saying that yours was their perfect job, wouldn't you give them a few minutes of your time? Remember, this is their perfect job, not necessarily yours."

Ann said, "Well, I guess if they were that passionate about it and really wanted to chat, I would certainly spend some time talking about my job. It might not be that exciting for me, but I can see how it could help them. I might be concerned that they might take my job though."

"I understand that," said Chris, "however, if you feel secure in your role you would probably make the time, wouldn't you?"

"Yes, I guess I would," said Ann.

"If I understand this correctly, Chris," said Carlos, "what you're saying is that the perfect job is out there, but you need to go after it because it won't just fall from the sky. Correct?"

"Yes, precisely. Here's another example," Chris continued, "when I graduated from school, I really wanted to be a radio personality. At that age, I didn't even know why I took a business degree in university. I had always dreamed of being a DJ on the radio growing up. So, I called the morning guy at the biggest radio station in the city to tell him about my desire to get into radio and I asked him if I could meet with him. I told him my story about my dreams of wanting to become a DJ and how I would really be grateful if he could spend a few minutes with me. My gut told me I was never going to meet this guy and that he wouldn't make the time for a kid like me. To my surprise, he agreed to meet! I met him the following week for about an hour and he told me the true ins and outs of the broadcasting industry. He was a great guy and a great source of information about the industry. He told me that the radio business was really competitive and that you can get fired at any time when you're in broadcasting. He told me that radio stations have consultants that come in to the stations, tell management that the station needs to change formats to maintain or grow their listener base. This results in 'staffing changes', also known as terminations, for their radio personalities. That meeting turned me off from getting into radio at the time, although I still think one day I will try to do it. It was a real eye-opener learning that side of the business. I realized it wasn't the perfect job for me anymore."

"I'm too shy to do that," said Ann.

"If you want your perfect job, it's not going to be easy," said Chris. "You're going to have to get out of your comfort zone. If you can't pick up the phone to call someone who can help you get that perfect job, you won't get there. It will be a huge benefit to you to call people who are where you want to be and ask them questions. Meet with them. Talk about what they like and don't like. Ask them how you can get to where they are? Share your list with them. Show them your passion. Do you know what the best thing is that will come out of it?"

"They'll help you get there?" said Ann.

"Of course!" said Chris. "There will be some people who won't want to help, but most people generally like to help others. As long as they're not threatened that you'll take their job away, I'm sure they will give you some time!"

Carlos said, "I'm definitely not afraid of picking up the phone to call someone if it will get me ahead. I just never thought about writing up a list like that. Most of my opportunities that I've had over the years have just come to me. I never thought about going after something like this. This is tremendous advice. Thanks for sharing this concept."

Chris replied, "My pleasure."

Ann asked Chris, "Any other advice on this topic?"

Tales from the Recruiter

Chris answered, "Just a few more things. First is that it will take time to come up with your list, longer to come up with the perfect job, and even longer to find that perfect job. You're going to need a lot of patience and plan for a lot of time to do all three steps, possibly even months. However, it will be worth it if you can ultimately find that perfect job. Second, your perfect job today may not be your perfect job in the future as your life, personality and needs change. Third, you should periodically update your list, and compare not only new opportunities that come up, but your existing position against your list. If a new job opportunity meets less than 80% of what's on your list, you should not pursue the position. If your current position meets less than 80% of what's on your list, it might be time for you to start looking for another position. If it's more than 80% of your list, you're on the right track."

"Makes sense," said Carlos.

Raj sighed. "Right now I'm just looking for a job. Anything…"

Chris said, "Something will come… just be patient. Have you made a list like what I'm suggesting?"

Raj shook his head.

Chris said, "Perhaps that could be your homework." Raj agreed.

The four spent a few more minutes chatting about what they were going to be doing the upcoming weekend before calling it a night.

CHRIS' THREE POINTERS:

1. Think of what would be on your list of things that would make your 'perfect job'.

2. Determine the position that would meet as many, if not all, of the things on your list.

3. Go after that position – volunteer if you're not qualified.

CHAPTER SIXTEEN

"HOW DO I DECIDE WHICH JOB TO TAKE?"

$\mathbf{A}$s the four sat down together that Wednesday they talked about the opportunities Raj had recently been interviewing for. Raj had been on a couple of interviews and was encouraged with one of the positions in particular.

Carlos also mentioned that he heard about an opportunity with a company through a friend, but he hadn't heard back as yet as to a possible interview. Although he wasn't really looking for a new position, he had sent his resume in anyway.

"Sounds like the market might be picking up..." suggested Ann.

Carlos said, "Yes, it does seem like it."

Raj nodded his head and said, "It definitely seems that I'm hearing about more opportunities. Also, thanks to Chris' help I'm able to understand the Canadian job market a little more."

Chris said, "It's my pleasure. Anything I can do to help. I know a lot of recruiters who wouldn't spend the time that I'm spending with you, but I feel that one day you will be able to help me with something – not sure what, or when, but one day..."

Ann said, "I'm sure that will happen. I also want to thank you, Chris."

"No problem!" said Chris. "By the way, I'm also noticing a pickup in the number of open jobs that are out there. Recruiters usually have a good pulse on how the job market is doing since they're in touch with candidates and clients all the time. It's a pretty simple equation. Generally speaking, the more calls recruiters get from people looking for jobs the worse the economy is getting. The more calls recruiters receive from companies looking to fill the positions the better the economy is getting. As such, recruiters usually have a good sense of how the job market is doing at any particular time."

"That makes a lot of sense," said Ann.

Chris asked, "Does anyone have any questions for this week?"

"I do!" said Carlos. "We've been asking you a lot of questions each week.

I'm wondering if there are any topics that we haven't asked you about that you think we should. Anything that we haven't talked about so far, that you think would be good for us to know or perhaps one of your favourite topics?"

Chris said, "Well, thanks for the opportunity to go over a topic of my choice! I always have lots of topics that I love talking about, but one thing we haven't talked about is multiple offers. For example, if I had two or more job offers at once, how do I decide on which job to take?"

"I was in that situation a few years ago." said Carlos.

"How did you handle it?" asked Chris.

"I accepted the position where I thought my career would take off faster," said Carlos.

"That's good," said Chris. "I would suggest taking a very systematic approach to deciding which job to take if you're ever in that situation. I'm a little more detailed when it comes to major decisions, like accepting one offer over another. Taking a job can be a significant life and career-changing decision. You need to take it seriously. Most people tend to bounce from job to job and usually take a position because an opportunity becomes available. Many people accept the first offer they receive because it's usually the only one available. If they're not working, their choice is to accept the position, and start making money, or not work. Most people will take the job, but not because they necessarily really want it or it's best for their careers. Sometimes people don't take a job offer because employment insurance pays more than the opportunity."

"I suppose you're going to say that if you had an up-to-date list of everything about your perfect job it would be easy to check the opportunities that come up against your list?" joked Ann.

"Of course!" smiled Chris. "That's the easiest way of determining whether an opportunity is in line with what you're really looking for in a position. Again, if a position doesn't meet at least 80% of that list, it's probably not the right opportunity. Some people take a job that they would rank seven out of 10 and then don't last in the position. They either start looking again for another position, never stop looking for something new, and/or dread going to work every day. I've seen many people like that. That starts a downhill process whereby they begin to dislike going to work and then their motivation declines. Ultimately they start looking for another job, or get terminated. I've seen so many resumes over the years of people who have one job for six months, then another for 18 months, then three months, etc. I firmly believe that everyone can find a perfect job, or close to it, if they put their minds to it and work at it. I know it's not easy, but the payoff is amazing! If you find that perfect job, it won't feel like you're working. You'll love what you're doing."

"That's very inspiring," said Ann. "You also wanted to talk about multiple offers. Is the perfect job what you mean about 'multiple offers'?"

"Actually, no…" said Chris, "multiple job offers is a situation where you have two or more job offers at the same time and you need to decide which of those two or more positions to take. Perhaps one of those offers is your perfect job!"

"I would only be so lucky to have multiple offers," sighed Raj.

"You may one day, Raj!" said Chris. "You never know. Carlos mentioned that he had multiple offers."

"Yes, but that's Carlos – he's a star," said Raj.

Carlos smiled.

Chris explained, "It doesn't matter. Anyone can have multiple offers at some point in their careers. As such, you should be prepared to think about how you're going to decide on one of those two or more job offers. There are at least four possible ways you can look at analyzing multiple offers:

1. As I already mentioned, one way is by first comparing your list to that perfect job to see if any of the offers meets at least 80% of what you're looking for. You can then reject anything below that 80%, because you won't ultimately be happy with a position that's less than 80% of your list.

2. A second way is to make a list of all the positives for each of the job offers that you receive. For example, on your list of positives, you could include things like salary, benefits, career growth potential, training provided and stability of the company. Do this for each opportunity that you have. By doing these lists, it may become

161

clearer to you as to which opportunity you should take, and which makes the most sense because it has the most positives.

3. In the third method, you can take each of the most important things to you, and assign points based on how important they are for you. For example, you could assign a maximum of 10 points for location (that is, how long it would take you to get to work and back each day), five points for your potential co-workers (for example, how you think you would get along with them), 15 points for career advancement (what opportunities you might have to grow in your career), etc. From there, you score each aspect of each job based on the maximum score available for each aspect.

As such, your scoring may look like the following (Chris drew a chart on the whiteboard):

Description	Maximum Points	Job #1	Job #2
Location	10	8	6
Co-Workers	5	5	4
Career Advancement	15	13	15
Etc.			
Totals	**120**	**106**	**85**
Percentage of Maximum Points	100%	88%	71%

You then add up the total for each job and you divide that by the total of the "Maximum Points" to come up with a percentage. Again, if that number isn't more than 80%, it's probably not the right role for you in the first place. In this example, job #2 might not be the right job for you because it's only 71% of your maximum score. The job that has the higher percentage, all things being equal, is the job that you should probably be leaning towards."

Chris continued, "Once you finish your scoring, you might want to go for a walk, go do something else for a few hours or even a day or two, and then come back to review your scoring to make sure that your point scoring made sense. For example, upon looking at your list again, you might revise your score for location to 15 points as a maximum score because you have children. You realize that being close to home is just as important at this point in your life as, say, career advancement. Any questions on this scoring?"

Ann asked, "Yes, how do you decide the rating scale? For example, why 15 and not 150 points?"

Chris said, "You can decide whatever the value is for each point. It's subjective. It's what you decide. The maximum score should be relative to each other in terms of importance."

"Oh okay, I understand," said Ann.

"Any other questions?" asked Chris.

Raj asked, "In your second way, you suggested writing down the positives for each position. What about the negatives of the positions?"

Chris said, "The negatives of one position should be the positive of the other position. For example, if one position is farther than the other, which is a negative for you, the other position will have the positive of being closer to you. The negatives of one position should be the positive of the other, so just note the positives. All points should show as positives. It doesn't always work perfectly, but should work for this exercise. Does that make sense?"

Raj nodded.

Carlos said, "You mentioned there were four ways, but you've only mentioned three so far."

Chris continued, "You're right Carlos. I didn't forget! The last choice, which most people who are working might not think of, is the option of staying where they are. Sometimes people are so definite on making a move to find another job because of something that's happening with their current position that they forget about all the positives about staying where they are. You should have another column in your ranking to score your existing position. What score would you give your current position, based on salary, location, career advancement, etc.? There are certainly benefits of staying where you are. If you've been at a job for less than two years, for example, a positive of staying where you are is to show stability on your resume. That is worth something, especially if you take a new job and it doesn't turn out the way you expected it to be and you start looking for another position again. In that situation, your resume would show that you were at a job for less than two years, then another job of only a few months and then you're looking again. Recruiters tend to place people who are stable in their work experience. They don't like job seekers who are jumpy in their jobs, because it is a red flag."

"Because of their guarantees on the placements, right?" asked Carlos.

"There's that, but recruiters want to do a good job for their clients," said Chris. "A recruiter's reputation is important. Recruiters don't want to place someone in a position and then that person leaves after three months. As such, staying where you are is also an option. I like to call this the 'do nothing' option. Just because one or more job offers are in front of you, no one is telling you that you have to take one of those. You can stay where you are, unless of course there is a reason that you have to find something else. For example, a situation where you know you will be losing your job at a certain date or you're finishing a contract. So all in all, keep in mind that you should consider staying with your current job if another opportunity isn't better than where you are now. Remember, the grass isn't always greener on the other side. Perhaps by changing some aspects of your current position you might be able to improve your ranking of it. Having a chat with your manager about your concerns in your current position can sometimes work wonders. It's less common that someone leaves a job because of their salary or benefits – as such, sometimes aspects about your current job can be changed if you are vocal about any issues that you're having."

Ann said, "I don't know if I can stay at my current job even if I speak with my boss. He just doesn't listen to me."

Chris responded, "If your job gets to a point where you can't stand to be there anymore, you know it's time to leave. Sounds like you might be at that point Ann. It's the point of no return – it's the point where you need to find something new because turning back is mentally impossible. I've been there. I think we all have at some point. It's quite natural."

Ann nodded in agreement.

Carlos asked, "Chris, how long would you suggest staying at a job?"

Chris said, "That is a very broad question. There are so many variables. For example, generally speaking I would expect a CEO of a major public corporation to be at their position for a number of years. On the other hand, I'd generally expect someone in a collections role to be changing jobs more frequently, because of the turnover rates of that type of position."

Ann pointed out, "A friend of mine in collections has been at her company for over 20 years."

Chris said, "Yes, that's why I generalized. I know I shouldn't do that, but how long someone stays in a position depends on a number of factors including the person, their personality, their education, their title, sometimes luck, who they report to, what their responsibilities are, etc. I've seen people that have been lucky. They have found an employer and a job that they really love and they never want to leave. One thing I can say is that recruiters get turned off by someone who is too jumpy in their roles. I've seen resumes of people with seven jobs in the last five years. They get downsized, they only get contracts, they are restructured out of their positions, etc. They seem to always be in the wrong place at the wrong time – they were let go after a three month contract, the company had financial difficulties and they were dismissed, the company had to downsize and they were the one that was selected, etc. That's what they'll tell you, but you're only hearing one side of the story. It's always someone else's fault. It's never their fault. People like that can be a recruiter's potential nightmare. I stay away from those people. I like dealing with candidates who are stable in their work experience, staying at jobs a very minimum of two years. From a recruiter's perspective, seeing people who are at each of their jobs for at least three years is good. It's like dating – how interested are you in someone who you start dating who has had three boyfriends or girlfriends in the last seven months?"

They all laughed.

Chris laughed, "I don't know if Ann would be interested in dating that kind of guy!"

Ann shook her head and smiled.

Chris continued, "In recruiting, that candidate is potentially trouble for recruiters."

Raj asked, "What about someone new to Canada, like me, who might need to do some temporary work or contracts just to get some experience?"

"That's different..." explained Chris, "that is completely understandable. If you're doing some short term temporary or contract positions just to get some experience in Canada after arriving, it will be apparent on the resume. I'm talking about someone who has been in Canada for a long time, and yet still is jumpy in their roles. I'm not saying that they might not have had some personal issues or valid reasons of why they had so many jobs, or that they wouldn't be able to ever find a job again. All I'm saying is that when they come to a recruiting firm, it's a more difficult type of candidate for recruiters like me to place with my clients."

"That makes sense," said Carlos. "I know at our company we really look at *why* people left their last few jobs when we're interviewing them and anything that doesn't make sense, we'll turn away."

"It's very important to build a solid resume and show stability in the jobs that you're working in," explained Chris. "You will create more value and, generally, you will earn more in compensation because of your loyalty to your previous employers. I once hired a person to work for me, let's call her Gina, who talked a good talk during the interviews about her stability and loyalty to her previous employers. She quit four or five months after she started with me. Her explanation of why she was quitting was that she had to go overseas for a family emergency, and gave me one day's notice instead of the usual two weeks. I later found out that her 'family emergency' was a one week trip down to the Caribbean with her boyfriend, and that the day after she got back from her vacation she started a position with another recruiting firm. She ended up there for about a year before she either got fired or quit for something else. Definitely someone I wouldn't recommend. One day it's going to haunt her because someone is going to realize that she worked for me and they will call me to get a reference on her."

"You sound like you're looking forward to that day," suggested Carlos.

Chris explained, "I mean, I don't wish anyone harm... but don't lie about a 'family emergency' that's really a trip down south with your boyfriend. I would have had more respect for her had she just told me the job wasn't for her, and asked for permission to leave right away. I would have given her that without a doubt."

"Makes sense," said Ann.

"You do have all kinds of stories about people, Chris," commented Carlos.

"Too many to talk about," laughed Chris. "When you're dealing with people, there are always stories, both good and bad. Walk a week in my shoes, and you'll know what I mean. Some of the stuff you see, you would just shake your head at."

"Great meeting!" said Ann. "This has given me a lot to think about my current job. Maybe I should stick around longer. There are some good things about where I work, and I suppose I shouldn't dismiss those. They do have a pretty good benefits plan which I like. I'm going to make a list of the things I like about my current job and see where that takes me."

"Good idea!" said Chris. "You might not dislike it as much as you think. Remember that the grass isn't always greener on the other side!"

"True enough," said Ann.

The four finished their meeting for the week.

CHRIS' THREE POINTERS:

1. Evaluate multiple offers based on criteria that are important to you.

2. Weigh the criteria based on their importance to you.

3. There's always the 'do nothing' option – decline other opportunities and stay where you are.

CHAPTER SEVENTEEN

"SHOULD I GO TO JOB FAIRS?"

"**A**ny good stories so far this week?" asked Carlos, as the four sat down for their meeting.

"I had an interview with a small company for a junior engineering position," answered Raj. "It was okay, nothing special."

"What was wrong?" asked Ann.

"Well, I didn't really think I clicked with the interviewer," said Raj. "He seemed a little too direct, didn't really give me a chance to answer the questions that he asked, and the interview only lasted about 20 minutes. I prepared a lot for the interview. I researched the company, thought about how I was going to answer questions and made a list of the questions I wanted to ask. It was such a short interview - I don't know what happened. I thought I was a good match for the role. I spent more time getting dressed and taking a shower than the actual interview!"

Chris asked, "How did it end?"

Raj said, "He just said that he would get back to me if they were to go to the next step."

Ann said, "That's terrible."

Raj sighed, "Yes, it didn't feel too good. Seemed like a waste of time to go."

Chris said, "You know, sometimes companies don't realize the bad reputation that they get by either having very short interviews with candidates or when they interview hundreds of people for a position looking for that perfect candidate. Word gets out quickly about those companies and then people don't want to work there. I have one client like that. They probably interview about 50-60 people for each job - some interviews are short, some are long, but they never hire anyone because they always think there's a better candidate out there. This goes on for months."

"You're kidding, right?" asked Carlos.

Chris replied, "No, that's what they do. And then when we call other candidates telling them about the position, they'll ask if it's Company X.

When we tell them that it is, they say that they don't want to go for an interview there because they've heard bad things about the company. Their friends have gone for interviews there and they don't want to go there. Companies don't understand how they're harming themselves by doing that. One more thing I would say about this situation is that you never know, Raj – you might end up getting called back for another interview."

"Why do you say that?" asked Raj.

"Well," Chris began, "when a client interviews my candidates for their positions, they will interview about five or six candidates and then think one or two candidates are the front runners; however, as they meet the candidates a second or even third time sometimes their initial lower-ranked candidate might move higher on the list, and sometimes that person ends up getting the job."

"How does that happen?" asked Ann.

Chris answered, "Sometimes someone moves up the ranking because the job requirements or skills needed for the position change during the interview process. Maybe a job seeker brings up something about their background in a second interview that was missed in the first interview. Sometimes one of the top-ranked candidates gets another job before the client is ready to make an offer or other times the top candidate's salary expectations are above what the company is looking to pay. The bottom line is that you never know. It didn't sound good with only a 20 minute interview, Raj, but wait and see."

"I'm always hopeful," said Raj.

"Follow-up with a thank you letter and stay positive," continued Chris. "Sometimes you'll be surprised. I hired someone recently who was initially my third-ranked candidate. My first pick's references were terrible when I called them and I decided that my second-ranked candidate wasn't the right person either after she met with our HR manager. She sensed that the second-ranked candidate had a bit of a negative attitude, by saying some negative things about their previous boss. So candidate number three got the job and he has worked out great so far."

"I never thought that could happen," said Raj.

"Yes it can. It does all the time," said Chris. "So keep that in mind, stay positive. Things happen."

The others nodded their heads.

"What should we discuss today?" asked Chris.

Raj put up his hand and looked at the others to make sure no one else had anything pressing. Everyone looked at Raj.

Raj said, "There's a big job fair coming up tomorrow downtown. I hear it's a wonderful opportunity to meet companies, but I don't really know too much about them as I've never been to one. I don't know how they work or whether it's worthwhile for me to go. So Chris, perhaps you can answer the question as to whether I should go? If so, what should I do when I'm there?"

Ann asked, "Raj, are you talking about the job fair that's happening at the Convention Centre?"

Raj nodded. "Yes."

Ann said, "I was thinking about going to it also. Maybe we can go together. It seems like there are some big companies who are going to be participating. I'd also be interested in attending and hearing what I should do to prepare."

Chris said, "That's a great topic to cover this week. Unfortunately I can't go to that job fair tomorrow; I would have liked to go to check it out. It gives me an idea of which companies are hiring and trends in the recruiting industry. Make sure to tell me how it goes at our meeting next week."

Raj replied, "Absolutely."

Chris began, "There's a lot to cover about job fairs. Companies will have tables or displays set up, will promote their companies as places to work and take resumes from job seekers. Some jobs fairs are big and some are small. Some job fairs have hundreds of companies while others might just be put on by one company. Job fairs are different from trade shows. Trade shows are typically used for a company to promote their products or services to buyers. Job fairs are primarily intended for companies to find people for their open positions and for job seekers to meet potential employers."

"There are positives and negatives for job seekers to go to job fairs," continued Chris. "Some of the benefits of going to a job fair are that they let you find out what companies are hiring, you can speak with recruiters that work for those companies and you can be in front of people that could help you in finding a position. A company will spend quite a bit of time and money to participate in job fairs, to showcase their organization as a preferred employer, and to find candidates for open positions. If you're the right fit for one of those positions, you might stand a better chance of getting the job than if you never met the representatives. Recruiters at the job fairs who receive resumes sometimes put little stars on the resumes of candidates that are good after they meet to make sure that they follow-up with them later."

"What kind of companies go to these job fairs?" asked Raj.

Chris answered, "Oh, all kinds. There could be smaller companies who might only be looking to fill one position. There may be larger companies who may have multiple positions to fill and need a lot of people. Schools or training organizations could be there to promote their educational programs for people who are looking to upgrade their skills. Government organizations may be there to highlight free services that they might provide to job seekers or those looking to start a new business. There are companies that may be there who look for people to sell their products, like life insurance. Those types of companies may only offer commission-only type roles, with no guaranteed salary. Professional organizations, like accounting or HR associations, may also attend – they are looking to raise awareness of the associations or to get new members to join. There may also be recruiting firms or staffing agencies looking for candidates for their clients. You might also meet resume writers or coaches who can give you feedback on your resume and tell you what changes you should make."

"That sounds great. How much does it cost to have your resume reviewed? How much does it cost to get in to these job fairs?" asked Ann.

"Typically, there's no charge for getting in to a job fair or getting your resume reviewed," said Chris. "Sometimes there is a small charge for job seekers to attend, but not that often. The coaches or resume writers that are there want to get their name out there and maybe get some business down the road. They offer free resume reviews and then charge later if someone wants a more thorough review. Not all job fairs will have coaches or resume writers but, when they are, there are sometimes long lineups to meet with them," said Chris.

"Who do the companies pay to participate in these job fairs and how much does it cost them?" asked Carlos.

Chris replied, "Organizers of the job fairs charge companies to be there. They arrange for the companies to have tables, sometimes include lunch for the exhibitors, advertise the job fair to job seekers, etc. The costs to put on a show for the organizers can be high. As for how much the companies are charged, it really depends on the size of the job fair and how much advertising the organizers do. Some job fairs are actually free for companies to participate in as sometimes the government pays the organizers to put on the job fair."

"How do I know what companies will be at the job fair? How do I know if there are going to be resume writers there?" asked Raj.

"You should check any marketing materials of the job fair to see if they are advertising who will be there and what kinds of positions those companies might be looking to fill," said Chris. "There may be some information somewhere as to which companies will be there. There might also be presentations from people who are in the recruiting industry that might be interesting for you to listen to. You can find out what time they are going to be there."

"You mentioned earlier that there were potential disadvantages of going to a job fair," mentioned Raj. "What would those be?"

"Well, for one thing," replied Chris, "job fairs can sometimes be very crowded and very noisy. When they are, you might not be able to really speak with a recruiter for long as you'd like as there might be a long lineup at their booth or the noise might make it hard to hear. Another thing is that you might spend a lot of time preparing for the job fair, getting ready, making copies of your resume and get there only to find out that there really aren't any positions that you're looking for. Maybe the job fair specializes in one area like healthcare, engineering, or accounting."

"I'll take an engineering job!" smiled Raj.

"Yes, I know," smiled Chris. "All I'm saying is that you should try to find out, if you can, what kind of jobs they might have available before you go so you won't be disappointed. Those would be the major negatives about going to a job fair. But overall, it can be very beneficial. At job fairs, if you connect at the perfect time, a recruiter might actually interview you on the spot for an open position. That can be a pretty direct way to a job. One exhibitor that I spoke to that came to one of our job fairs said they hired 15 people from it."

"You organize job fairs?" asked Raj.

"Yes," said Chris, "we organize, promote and manage job fairs throughout the city. We have one coming up in a few months also. I'll let you know when we have it."

"What should someone do when they approach a booth?" asked Ann.

Chris replied, "Ask the company what kind of positions they are looking to fill. Have copies of your resume ready to give them if they have a position or positions relevant to your background. If they have a position along the lines of what you're looking for, give them a short commercial about yourself, maybe 20-30 seconds of who you are, what you're looking for, and see how the conversation goes from there. They might just take your resume back to the office so they can review it later or sometimes they'll ask you to have an interview with them right then and there. In the case of a training centre or school, they'll tell you about the programs that they provide, so you don't really need to give them your resume. What happens at the booth will depend on the organization, the recruiter, etc. Don't just give out your resume without having an idea first about the types of jobs they have. You should also be careful about who you give your resume to since it contains your personal information. Just because there's a booth at a job fair doesn't mean that the company is reputable - all that means is that a company has registered to be there. The organizers of the job fairs don't always make sure that the exhibitors are reputable. There's no harm in being a little skeptical."

"Is there a better time of day to go to a job fair?" asked Raj.

"I would try to go to the fair when it's less busy, personally," said Chris. "Earlier is better, as later in the day the people at the booths get tired. It's fairly exhausting for the exhibitors to be at the job fairs. Most of the time they're standing on their feet all day talking to people. By the end of the day, they're just looking to go home so try to stay away from the later hours. I would also try to stay away from lunch hours since it can be busier at that time."

"Chris, you always have funny stories about these things – anything about job fairs that you want to share?" asked Ann.

"Well, I think one of my favourite stories," said Chris, "are the candidates who come to the booths and say things like 'What are you going to do for me?' or 'What do you have for me?' Those people should think about what they can do for the organization, not the other way around."

"They should learn about networking and first offering to help someone else!" pointed out Carlos.

"Precisely," said Ann.

"You're all learning," Chris smiled. "I don't understand if those job seekers just don't understand the purpose of job fairs, or if they are just so self-centered that they don't realize they should be trying to sell themselves to a company first. Completely rude! They will have zero chance of getting hired. With that kind of attitude, they might as well stay home and not bother going to the job fairs. You should be pleasant, have a smile on your face and not be arrogant. Be humble when you meet the recruiters. Act just like you would when you meet someone for an interview. Be professional and dress the part. When we're done today I'm going to give you a copy of some of my tips on what to do before, during and after the job fair."

"That would be great," said Raj. "Anything else you can tell us?"

"The tips that I will give you will help, but also make sure to eat before you go to a job fair," said Chris. "Sometimes the job fairs have limited food choices, if at all. It's always a good idea to eat beforehand so you're fresh. A couple of other things – one is that sometimes there are exhibitors there who are just trying to promote their organizations and aren't actively trying to recruit anyone. They are just there to make sure that potential job seekers know about their organizations. Another thing is that sometimes recruiters will make notes on your resume so that they'll be able to remember the better candidates they had met. Oh, and one other thing... if you really want to impress a recruiter, find out beforehand what companies are going to be there, or even the exact name of the person, and put a covering letter with that name or names, company name and address of that organization. That would really make you stand out when you meet them, and would be more memorable for the recruiters later. It requires a bit of work to do this, but it may give you an edge over other candidates."

"This is excellent information, Chris," said Raj.

"Thanks," said Chris. "Carlos, you've been pretty quiet through most of this. What are you thinking?"

"This is all great information – thanks Chris," said Carlos. "While you were speaking I was thinking of two things – one is: I wonder if it would be good for me to go to the job fair with Ann and Raj tomorrow. And secondly, I'm wondering whether it would make sense for our company to have a booth at a job fair also. I know our company is always looking for some IT people, so I wonder if it might make sense for our company to be there also."

"Similar to job seekers going to job fairs," said Chris, "there are also pros and cons of a company having a booth at a job fair. It's probably too late for your company to be there at tomorrow's job fair, but it might be a good idea for your company to consider attending other job fairs. You and I can talk about that separately if you'd like. You might want to go to the job fair also just to see what it's about."

"Sure, that would be good," said Carlos.

The four realized that it was time to wrap up their meeting, but before everyone left, Chris made copies of his tips about job fairs and gave one to each person (*Appendix 11*).

CHRIS' THREE POINTERS:

1. Find out ahead of time what organizations will be at a job fair.

2. When speaking with an exhibitor at a job fair, make sure to listen, ask questions and not do all the talking.

3. Follow-up with any organizations that might have the types of positions you are qualified for.

CHAPTER EIGHTEEN
"WHAT ARE YOUR TOP RECRUITER SECRETS?"

At the beginning of the next meeting, the four talked about the job fair that Ann and Raj attended the previous week. Ann and Raj did go to the fair but Carlos couldn't make it. Chris asked them what they thought of it.

"It was fairly busy," said Raj, "I didn't realize there were so many people looking for jobs in the city. I was able to speak with a few organizations and I did give my resume to a few people, but I haven't heard anything back yet."

"It does take time for recruiters to go through all the resumes after a job fair," said Chris. "Sometimes we come back to the office with 500-1,000 resumes after a big event."

"I understand," said Raj, "I think Ann had something maybe come up last week."

"Yes, I did!" said Ann. "I met with one organization that interviewed me right there for a position. They said they will get back to me this week, but I haven't heard anything back yet."

"Well, good luck to both of you," said Chris.

"Thanks for your advice, Chris," said Ann. "I never would have known a lot of this stuff had we not met."

"I'm happy to help," said Chris. "I didn't know a lot about the recruiting business and how recruiting worked before I got into the industry. I think people have a general idea on how jobs are found and what recruiters do, but sometimes people have a huge expectation of what recruiters do and how they can help. I've met some people who think that recruiters can guarantee everyone they meet any job that they want. It just isn't the case. In fact, one statistic that I've generally heard in the recruiting industry is that only about one out of every seven people that a recruiter interviews actually gets a job through that recruiter. That's not great odds if you think about it!"

"That is quite low... I didn't realize that," said Carlos.

Chris replied, "Yes, it is low. That's why you want to improve your odds as much as possible. Don't limit yourself to *only* working with recruiters

– cast the net as widely as possible."

Ann commented, "Ok, Chris. I understand. You've told us a lot of things behind the scenes of things to do, but you must also have some secrets that can help us get a job through recruiters. Do you have any top recruiter secrets that we haven't talked about yet?"

"I sure do!" smiled Chris. "I love sharing secrets about the industry and what you can do to improve your chances of getting a job. Let's take a look behind the scenes, so to speak!"

"These should be good," said Raj.

"First of all, I've already mentioned bringing a list of your references to interviews," said Chris. "Bringing references shows that you're prepared to make a move and you're not just shopping around. Recruiters like to deal with candidates who are organized and have nothing to hide. It also shows you're prepared and organized. Make sure that you have confirmed with your references that you can list them. Bringing your references can really improve your chances of getting a job."

"What other secrets do you have?" asked Ann.

"Well, make sure you're using the right recruiting firm," said Chris. "In some cities and towns, there are a lot of different recruiting firms available for you to contact, so it's important to know which recruiting firms focus on your experience. If you send your resume to a recruiting firm that doesn't specialize in your area, your resume will probably end up being ignored."

"How can you know which firms are the right ones?" asked Ann.

"You can start by looking at the type of positions that they are advertising for," said Chris. "Are they advertising the types of jobs that you would be looking for? Call them and ask them what kinds of positions they generally recruit for. I know it can be time consuming, but it will save you time in the long run."

The others nodded.

Chris continued, "The next point is that in a perfect world, when recruiters are looking to fill a position, they are looking for people who have the same or very similar experience to the position for their client. Use that knowledge to your advantage by having a recruiter find you a job that you're most qualified for. Recruiters will be more interested in you if you have relevant experience to the positions they're looking to fill. Similarly, if you don't have relevant experience, it's very difficult to do a career change through a recruiter. It happens, but very rarely."

Chris added, "I want to repeat something that I've already mentioned, as I think this is very important - go after the job that you're looking for. Contact people in that role and ask them what it would take to get a job in that particular field. Go out and get the necessary experience. Ask questions. Think of it like that person who started in the mail room and worked their way up to the president's office. Be humble. Start with low expectations. Don't think any role is beneath you. If you really want something, it probably won't be easy to get there. It might be financially, physically and/or psychologically difficult and will take time. But stay focused on the long term goal of what you're looking at doing. Demonstrate that you're willing to do anything to get to where you want to go, and back up your words with actions."

"I understand," Ann nodded.

Chris added, "For example, I've met many interns who have wanted to get into the recruiting industry and are willing to work for free to get experience. If they're that passionate about it, they will work hard, show what they can do, treat an internship like a real job and they might just end up getting hired. Over the years I've hired many interns who have worked first on a voluntary basis because they didn't have relevant experience; they worked hard, and showed that they really wanted it. Those are my favourite type of people. They're willing to make sacrifices to get what they want."

"Good ideas," said Raj, "maybe I should start thinking about doing that."

"It might not be a bad idea..." said Chris, "I know it's tough, but if you really want it..."

"Any other secrets?" asked Carlos.

Chris continued, "I have a lot. Another one is that not all positions that recruiters work on are advertised. Recruiters have their clients that they deal with. Sometimes they advertise the opening and sometimes they don't due to confidentiality issues or time constraints. We talked about the hidden job market in the past, remember? Recruiters can and should be part of your network so you can tap into that hidden job market. Don't rely exclusively on recruiters though as part of your job search – they should only be a part of your network. There are some candidates who just rely on recruiters with their search, believing that sending their resumes to recruiters is all that's needed to find a job. While this may be true for some types of job seekers, for the majority of people, recruiters should be a part of their search process, but not the only part."

"Also," continued Chris, "whether you're actively or passively looking for a position, recruiters prefer candidates who stay in regular contact, return phone calls and emails when they leave messages. Most recruiters use databases that help them track and keep a history of when contact is made with candidates. If you stay in touch with recruiters, they will contact you with opportunities when you might least expect it. If you're not working, you should contact recruiters at most a few times a month to let them know of your status. Calling a recruiter every day — or even more than once a week — will be annoying and may stand in the way of him or her helping you in your search for a new job. If you are working, making contact once every one to two months is recommended to keep you on their 'radar'. Or you can ask the recruiters how often they would like to be contacted. Depending on the type of role you're looking for, you should stay in touch periodically so they don't forget you, but use your discretion. Also, don't only contact recruiters when you need something from them. As I had mentioned a few weeks ago, I know some people who only contact me when they're looking for a job – sometimes I won't hear from them for many years. Don't be like that. Stay in touch with recruiters just like you would friends. The more they know about you, the more likely they will call you about that opportunity you wouldn't have even known existed. This is all about networking."

"Do you get a lot of calls and emails?" asked Ann.

"I do and I really do try to reply to each one individually," said Chris. "It is difficult sometimes though because of the sheer volume I get. I do have one person who calls me regularly, maybe every four to six weeks, just to stay in touch. He tells me he will stay in touch and he notes it in his daytimer to contact me. He's someone that I would think of immediately when I'm looking to fill a position he's qualified for, because he'd be top of mind for me."

"Makes sense," said Ann.

Chris continued, "Some job seekers also seem to think that if they apply to every job a recruiting firm has advertised that somehow they will increase their chances of getting a job. In fact, it generally has the opposite effect. When recruiters see a candidate that applies to every job available, their credibility is questioned."

"I understand that..." said Carlos, "these are good. Any other tips you have?"

"Well," began Chris, "recruiters like dealing with candidates that are up-front and honest about their intentions for finding a job. Leaving out an important detail about your search because you think it will hurt your chances will not help you in the long run. Be honest and up-front about things, even if it's bad news. If you're going to be dealing with recruiters, it's best to think long-term with them and not just what's going to happen today. Perhaps they don't find you a position this time, but you never know what they might have down the road. However, being deceitful will not help you in the long run. Experienced recruiters have heard and seen many situations, and typically expect the unexpected when dealing with candidates. If you have bad news for the recruiter, share it with them right away. For example, you're not going to hurt a recruiter's feelings if you are not interested in a role a recruiter has presented you."

Chris continued, "Recruiters are people and have feelings too. Sometimes they're on a high from having just filled a position. Or they're on a low because someone they placed a month earlier just quit the job and they have to start a new search to find a replacement. Or they're frustrated in dealing with a certain situation. So their emotions could swing from day to day. I realize that on your end you may be frustrated trying to find a new position, but making a recruiter's life easier may also help you achieve your goal. If you ultimately get placed by a recruiter, send an email or thank you card to show your appreciation."

"Recruiters also like referrals!" continued Chris. "It may be that a recruiter can't help you because of your skills or background, but he or she would be interested in people you know. Helping out a recruiter today with a referral can give you an advantage in the long run by strengthening your relationship with that recruiter, as well as being able to help someone you know with their search. The recruiter doesn't need to use your name as a referral if you want the referral kept confidential."

"I hadn't even thought about referring someone to a recruiter," said Ann. "I guess, primarily because I wouldn't want to lose out on an opportunity because a friend of mine got the job that I wanted."

Chris replied, "You're right – you could lose out on an opportunity, but that would be fairly rare to happen. I think if you're meant to get the job you will."

Ann said, "I suppose."

"What other tips?" asked Raj, on the edge of his seat.

"Be accessible," answered Chris. "Recruiters are usually on a time-crunch to fill a position. Make sure the recruiters have your up-to-date contact information so that you will be accessible or be able to reply to them on a timely basis. Recruiters won't keep trying to reach you if you don't return messages promptly, or at all."

"There's a lot to know," commented Raj.

"Yes, there is, but the more you know about how recruiters work the better you'll be able to deal with them," said Chris.

"Here are a few more ideas:

Be early for interviews
Show professionalism and respect by being early for interviews, and. Recruiters will not work with candidates who are regularly late for their appointments.

Keep your word
If you have committed to something, make sure you keep your promise. For example, if you say you will get an updated resume or references to the recruiter, or will call someone by a specific date or time, follow through on these commitments or your relationship with the recruiter will be negatively impacted.

Dress appropriately

Make sure to dress appropriately for meetings with both the recruiter and their clients. When you go to one of the recruiter's client's site for an interview, you are representing not only yourself but the recruiter as well.

Don't put up walls

It's important to be direct about why opportunities presented by the recruiter aren't right for you. At the same time, however, recruiters don't like to work with candidates who focus on the negative. The more times you say no to an interview or reject an opportunity, the less likely recruiters will be to contact you in the future. Be flexible in your demands (e.g. salary, location, etc.) and try to minimize the number of roadblocks.

Avoid last minute negotiations

Recruiters don't appreciate it when an offer that meets a candidate's requirements is made and then the candidate wants to negotiate salary and/ or other terms of the agreement before signing. Be direct and honest at the beginning of the process to avoid catching the recruiter off guard when an offer is presented.

Don't play games

Avoid playing games with recruiters by not providing accurate information or by being unclear about your employment situation. Experienced recruiters can detect inconsistencies or information that doesn't make sense. This type of behaviour can significantly hurt your chances of getting a new job. It could also result in your file being blacklisted by a recruiter forever — recruiter's databases have an excellent memory!

Mention anything significant

If you have other employment opportunities that you're interviewing for, you should mention it to the recruiter. This is especially important if you're in the late stages of the interview process with one of their clients. It may actually increase your chances of being offered the position if they realize there are multiple companies pursuing you. Any other details that might be significant should be brought up as early as possible. For example, if you've booked a one month vacation to Europe, this shouldn't be brought up the day before you're leaving.

Speak clearly on the phone

Speak your name clearly and say your phone number twice slowly on any voice mail messages that you leave.

Tales from the Recruiter

Make sure your resume is up-to-date

Recruiters generally aren't professional resume writers and don't rewrite resumes for people. When you meet a recruiter you should have a resume that has your current up-to-date work experience and is in an appropriate format. Consult a professional resume writer prior to meeting with a recruiter if your resume needs work.

Know what you want

Recruiters prefer working with candidates who know what they're looking for (type of position, company, location, etc.). Take the time to think this through carefully before meeting with the recruiter. The more unclear you are about what you're looking for, the less attractive you are to a recruiter as it will make it more difficult for them to place you.

Trust your recruiter

If a recruiter has told you you're not appropriate for their client, accept it. You can push back, but do it in a professional manner. Recruiters typically know their clients well and understand what they're looking for in candidates. They also know you and what you're looking for. If they don't feel there's a fit, they won't put you forward. Remember, it's in the best interest of a recruiter to place someone with their client.

Other considerations

- Turn off your cell phone during interviews.
- Don't accept a counter-offer — most employees who accept counter-offers typically leave their employer within six months and the employee-employer relationship is usually not the same after accepting a counter-offer. A counter-offer is when you resign from your position to go to a new company and your current employer offers you more money or other incentives to stay with them instead of leaving.
- Allocate enough time for interviews — don't be rushed to leave. If you have time constraints, let recruiters know ahead of time.
- Don't be too pushy, arrogant or try to oversell yourself. A little humility goes a long way with recruiters. Check your ego at the door.

These are just a few more important tips to keep in mind," replied Chris.

"What about resigning from a job?" asked Ann.

"It's very easy," replied Chris, "prepare a short resignation letter that includes that you have found another position, thank your boss for the opportunity that the organization has given you, and let them know when your last day will be. Ask to meet with your manager privately. Give the required notice - usually two weeks as I've mentioned before. Your manager may be disappointed but should understand your reason(s). Keep it positive because you may want them to be your reference one day. I have a sample resignation letter (*Appendix 12*) that I can give you. Also, your manager or someone in HR might also do an exit interview with you."

"What's that?" asked Ann.

"It's a series of questions your employer will ask you to understand why you're leaving the company, what you liked or disliked about the company and your position, what you would have changed, etc.," explained Chris.

"This was a great meeting," said Raj.

"I would definitely agree with that, it really was. I feel more prepared now to work with recruiters," said Ann as Carlos nodded his head.

"Thanks for the feedback," said Chris.

At that point, the four ended their meeting for the night.

CHRIS' THREE POINTERS:

1. Spend time with those recruiters that have the most likelihood of placing you.

2. Stay in touch with recruiters regularly, whether you're actively looking for a position or not – build relationships with them.

3. Treat interviews with recruiters just like you would as if you're meeting their client.

CHAPTER NINETEEN

"SHOULD I START A BUSINESS?"

Chris started the week's meeting with another one of his stories.

"One of the more uncomfortable situations in my recruitment experience happened a few years ago in our office," Chris described. "The situation was that one recruiter in the office set up an interview with a job seeker, while another recruiter set up an interview with the job seeker's manager! Neither recruiter knew that interviews were scheduled at the same time in our office, but both of the job seekers showed up in the lobby of our office for their 10:00 a.m. interviews. To their surprise, they both saw each other there. Obviously both candidates, as well as both recruiters, were put into a very awkward situation. Both candidates felt extremely uncomfortable for their own reasons, of course. Luckily, they both were able to discuss the situation on a very professional basis (in our offices), and came to the conclusion that neither would tell anyone that the other was there as it could possibly impact both their careers with their existing employer. They kept it a secret until they both found jobs through us and then shared a laugh about it weeks later. It could have definitely blown up in a lot of faces, but it worked out alright."

Everyone shook their head in disbelief.

"So, what would you like to discuss today?" asked Chris.

Carlos said, "Chris, I've been thinking about my career and what I really want. I've been asking myself if I should start a business and wonder if now was the right time. What are your thoughts?"

Chris had an idea of where this was coming from. Carlos was very bright and confident in his ability and would be an excellent person for starting up his own business. However, there are lots of bright and confident people who become entrepreneurs only to fail months or years later for a number of possible reasons, including lack of financing, loss of motivation or changes in career plans.

Chris began, "Carlos, I am an entrepreneur myself and it's been one of the best things that I've done in my life. As I mentioned previously, it's the perfect job for me. If you're confident in your ability, know what you want, and have a strong desire to succeed, owning or running your own business can be one of the best choices you'll ever make in your life. It's much easier now than ever before to start a business because of all the tools and support available. Information is a lot easier to find then it used to be. Setting up a website is simple. The tax advantages of running a business, compared with being an employee, are significant. However, I've seen people think that being your own boss is all fun and games, you make a lot of money, and you can boss people around, but that's just not the case. Being your own boss is not easy. You need a thick skin and also have to have financial resources, whether it's from you or from others, to be able to pay for the start-up and on-going costs. There are so many factors in starting and running your own business that it's very important to plan ahead and make sure that it's the right step for you."

Chris continued, "Rather than looking for a position that meets at least 80% of what you're looking for, as I've mentioned before, if you're starting your own business you should be looking to match at least 95% of what's on your list. I think it really has to be so close to being the perfect role for you in your career that if it's not, you're going to be frustrated in what you're doing and you won't cut it for the long term. There are so many statistics of companies that don't make it to the first year, second year or fifth year of business. I think it's because people don't think things through properly, they don't plan for it, they don't know whether their product or service will sell, they don't understand basic accounting, etc. There are so many reasons a business will fail that it seems the odds are stacked against a business succeeding. However, to combat those negatives, there have to be some serious positives. Things like a strong drive, available financing, a crystal clear understanding of the product or service that you'll be selling or providing, a commitment to succeed, the ability to take no for an answer many times over, a strong sales ability, an ability to find people to offset your shortcomings, etc."

"I'm an entrepreneur at heart," Chris said. "I seem to have it in my blood. My dad was a veterinarian and ran his own veterinary clinic for more than 30 years. I saw him leave early for work every day and come home late, work every weekend, and take very little vacation. I would see the strain of work on his face every day when he came home, after having to deal with client concerns, employee issues, payroll, ordering inventory, accounting and a myriad of other details that consumed his whole life. He was trained as a veterinarian, but because he was running his own clinic he was responsible for everything. He wasn't a businessman. He wasn't an accountant. He wasn't a sales person. He was a veterinarian and learned all those other areas by trial and error."

"You're kind of scaring me, Chris…" suggested Carlos.

"I don't want to scare you, Carlos!" said Chris. "I'm suggesting that you really have to think about all the issues in starting up a business and do a lot of research. It's not for the faint of heart and it's not for someone who doesn't think things through. I've seen so many people just start a business that don't have the slightest clue about what it takes. For example, the guy who is at a party having a few drinks and comes up with the idea of starting up a bar because he always thought his life's mission was to own a bar. The bar is fun to run and successful for six months, but then there are the realities - the economy, staff turnover, inventory costs, etc. It gets harder to operate and is no longer fun."

Chris continued, "Take the woman who always wanted to own a flower shop, quits her administrative position and pours her family's life savings into opening that kind of store. She has no idea of the tremendous responsibilities of running such an enterprise, including paying rent and taxes, budgeting, working seven days a week, computer issues, what to charge for the flowers, dealing with banks, sales, etc. That's even before getting into what flowers to get for the store, inventory that goes bad quickly, etc. I wouldn't recommend getting into a business only because your boss made you angry one day or you wanted to start bossing people around. It's just not that easy. People have lost a lot of money from a split-second decision to open up a business. When you think you're done researching a possible venture, spend more time researching it. Plan to spend at least 6-12 months doing your research. Speak with people who are already there. It's well worth the time."

"Since I've been having such a hard time finding a position so far, I've also thought about possibly opening up a business, Chris," said Raj. "This is an eye-opener though. What other suggestions do you have?"

Chris answered, "Well, here are some more tips. First of all, think of why you want to start your own business. You may feel that something is missing in your current position, you may want to be your own boss, experience all the freedom and responsibility that goes with it, or perhaps you've been downsized. You need to be prepared for a long-term commitment to a business opportunity, so you want to ensure your reasons for starting up a business are strong."

"When I got into business on my own," Chris continued, "I was 40 years old. Coincidentally, studies have found that the average age to start up a business is about 40, which generally amounts to 15-20 years of work experience after graduating from college or university before embarking on this new path. It generally gives you enough experience to know what things companies do well and what they don't do well. This amount of time gives you a base level of confidence to realize there are sometimes multiple solutions to problems that come up. This experience also allows you to have worked with different types of people – complainers, aggressive, passive, problem solvers, introverts, extroverts, etc. – and different types of work environments – hostile, team-oriented, high or low turnover, etc. This enables you to know what kind of environment you'd like to create for your organization."

Chris added, "Is now the right time for you, Carlos or Raj? Do you have the experience necessary to make a successful transition? If you're going to run your own business, you should be at a point in your career where you don't need the support system that working for someone else brings, including a guaranteed paycheque. Trust me, if you start your own business you might be eating macaroni and cheese for dinner a lot more times than you think until your business starts taking off, which will most likely be longer than you think. You'll need to overestimate how much it's going to cost you to run your business, and underestimate how much revenue you're going to generate in your first few years. Most people think they're going to be millionaires in their first year of running their business. It just doesn't work that way."

"I have seen many of my friends start up a business and fail," said Ann.

"Yes," Chris said, "if it was easy everyone would be doing it. It's definitely not for everyone. Here are some other tips for you:

Do something you know

One of the worst mistakes you can make is to get into a business that you aren't familiar with. Get industry experience before you start a business so that you understand the business economics of the industry. How much is charged for the product or service that you are thinking about selling? What is the profit margin? How are returns or bad service handled? What is the market for your product or service? Is your product or service part of a fad whose demand will disappear in the short term so you'll need to come up with new ideas, or is it something that will be in demand for years to come? Can you sell your product or service at a high enough price that will generate adequate revenues to cover your expenses?

Do something you love

Make sure that you love the business you're getting into for 10, 20 or 30 years. Have a passion for it. If your heart isn't really into it, don't do it because you won't last and you won't have the passion to survive.

Talk to people about their experience

Talk to people in the industry and ask them for input. Let them know you're considering opening up your own business. Ask them questions such as:

- Where is the industry going?
- What changes are taking place within the industry?
- What do they like about the industry?
- If they had to do it all over again, what would they do differently?
- What product/service is lacking in the industry?
- How can they help you with your new business?

The information that you gain by doing this kind of research may be invaluable in helping you make the right decision.

Budget

Having a detailed monthly budget, like line-by-line revenues and expenses, for the first couple of years will help you stay focused on your business. You will need to know how much money to borrow and at what time periods you might have difficulties with cash flow.

Take your time and make sure that you include all expenses and include a buffer for additional expenses that you might not anticipate. As I mentioned earlier, overestimate your expenses and underestimate your revenues.

Plan to negotiate with suppliers on amounts and terms of payment on everything you need to buy. Purchase supplies when they're on sale. Don't be shy about asking 'What's the best price you can do?' Budget so that you can take advantage of any early payment discounts offered by your suppliers. Every penny you save can go back into your business or pay yourself a bigger salary. Make sure that if you have suppliers that they are trustworthy, reliable, and will deliver as promised. Get things in writing as much as possible.

Make sure your financing is in place

Where is the money required to finance your business going to come from? Is a bank loan necessary? Do you have a line of credit? Are there government programs available that you can get loans or grants from? Do you have savings? Can you borrow money from family or friends? You'll need to know these answers since cash flow is the life-blood for a company.

Strategic Plan

Work with a professional to write a proper, strategic business plan, including:

- What will I be selling and at what price?
- Who will my customers be?
- How much are they willing to pay for my product or service?
- Where will I be working?
- How long will it take to make a sale?
- How long will it take to get paid after I make a sale?
- Does the market need my product or service?
- What are my short-term and long-term goals?

Putting your plan on paper will allow you to really understand what your business is all about, as well as help clarify your goals. Also, if you need to borrow money, your lenders will want to see some kind of a plan. Have someone review your plan and point out holes in it. Be open to suggestions and criticism. Don't get defensive if someone views your business with a critical eye and brings up things that you don't want to hear.

Who can help you?

Do you have people that can help you grow your business? Are there family members who can help work in your business? Can friends give you advice and steer you in the right direction? Will people you know be able to refer business to you? Can you get a coach or someone who has been there to help you? Is there an accountant and/or lawyer who will be able to help you set up your business (e.g. decide whether to incorporate or not)? Any free or low-cost assistance you can get will benefit your business. Check government programs available, such as low-interest loans or grants.

Can you sell?

If you're not comfortable with prospecting for sales, who is going to get you customers? You need to think about this because if you don't have any customers, you're not going to get very far. You may need to take a course or read a book on selling if you have no experience and sometimes practical experience is the only way.

Anticipate issues

Think of as many issues or obstacles up-front and how you will handle them. Obviously unexpected events are going to happen, but planning for worst-case scenarios can help you when they come up.

Keep things simple

Don't overcomplicate your business. Don't try to be all things to all potential customers. Try to stay focused on one or two things that you can do better than anyone else. At the same time, be flexible in helping your clients with their needs. Be open to ways of improving your business. People and companies are willing to spend money if you can help them save time or money. Be prepared to change your service/product mix depending on the changing demands of your customers.

Start small

Many people think you need to do a big media blitz with a huge advertising campaign to get customers initially. However, at the outset, especially as you're trying to understand your business, rely on friends and family to give you referrals to help you get customers.

Don't think of turning back

Once you make the decision to start your own business, take away any option of turning back. Take the thought out of your mind. If you're going to go for it, go for it! Put all your energy into making your new business work and don't have any regrets. If you've done your research properly, you know what you're doing. Many people think that entrepreneurs make decisions quickly however, the opposite is true. Most successful entrepreneurs I know take their time and do significant research before making a decision, especially when it comes to as critical a decision as to whether to start up a business or not.

Be patient

"They didn't build Rome in a day." Your business will take time to develop – years, not weeks or months. You need to be prepared to manage your emotions, not to get too high if things go well and not get too low if things don't. You will probably have more bad days than good, especially in the early stages of your business.

You will most likely be working more hours than you think with little or no results at the outset. You need to make sure you're mentally and physically prepared for that before you start.

Get family buy-in

Ensure your spouse and/or family is supportive. Ask them to be patient while you get your new venture going.

Can you make decisions?

You will need to make your own decisions in running your business. If you've been in an environment where your boss has made all the decisions for you, you will need to quickly learn to start making your own decisions on everything from financial, operational, and administrative issues. Are you a decision-maker? Are you comfortable in this role?

Outsource

Think of outsourcing or partnering with others for work that is outside of your scope of work (e.g. accounting, administrative). Have others that are experts in their fields help you so you can stay focused on what you do best. Don't underestimate the importance of having an accountant help you with your business. Don't do it all yourself – focus on what you're best at and get others to fill in the gaps.

Consider a Franchise/Purchase of an Existing Business

There are many franchising options available that can help you get set up and started quickly. Explore these options also as these might better suit your style and give you the ability to work with people who already understand the business. In addition, exploring opportunities to purchase an existing business may be another way of getting your business off the ground more quickly."

"There is *a lot* to know and think about from the sounds of it!" said Carlos.

"Absolutely!" said Chris. "Running your own business requires more time than you think. The suggestions that I'm making are only the tip of the iceberg of what will be required for your business. Prepare to work more hours than when you work for someone else. Follow your instincts if you really want something. Many people, including your family members, will try to talk you out of it. However, if you follow your heart, you can definitely be rewarded. You must make up your own mind on this. If you really believe that being a business owner is what you want to do, then do it. Don't be afraid to follow your dream."

"Very inspiring and educational," said Carlos.

"There's a lot to run a business," replied Chris, "however, it can be something that you can build and will be rewarding beyond your dreams. Treat your business like having a baby. Plan for it, know what is required and know it's going to be a lot of work. Think of your business as a long-term investment. It's going to be tough, especially in the first few years before it begins having its own legs. You might not get much sleep at the beginning as you'll have lots to worry about and lots of things to do. You'll also be investing in something with an undefined future. However, if you stick with it, the rewards will come later."

With that, the meeting ended. This turned out to be their last Wednesday meeting. Raj, Carlos and Ann all felt that they had covered a lot of topics over the last few months and were well on their way to finding that perfect opportunity. They no longer believed that they needed to meet regularly. The three thanked Chris for the information he had provided over the weeks and they all agreed to stay in regular contact with each other.

CHRIS' THREE POINTERS:

1. Your perfect 'job' might be to create your own by starting your own business.

2. Follow your dreams.

3. Do your research.

EPILOGUE

As you have read, there are a number of things to think of when searching for a job, ranging from your resume, cover letters, interviewing, networking, thank you letters, and the list goes on.

I hope that you have been able to get some help from my insights into the job and career world from my many years in the recruiting industry. As I mentioned in the preface, I wanted to keep this book as easy to read as possible with the goal of its being useful for as wide a variety of people as possible. As I have realized from having interacted with thousands of job seekers over the years, people across the whole spectrum of experience face many of the same issues, regardless of their backgrounds.

My favourite chapter I wrote in this book was the one called "Is there a perfect job?" and I wanted to touch on it again here. Most of the material in this book you can learn – how to do your resume, improving your interview skills, etc.

However, I believe that if you *really* want to be thrilled in your job or career, whatever that means for you, you have to find something that you love and that requires work – there are no shortcuts.

You need to understand what you're looking for in order to be able to find that perfect job or career, and work hard to go after it. It's not an easy process and it won't happen in 20 minutes. If you read about the background of any famous superstar, you'll find someone who worked extremely hard to get to where they are. I'm certain they faced tremendous hurdles and the odds were against them, including critics, friends, and family members who along the way said they would never make it. However, they also dreamed over and over again that they would succeed.

Be sure to set reasonable expectations– you're not going to become famous in a week. Similarly, you're probably not going to become the CEO of the largest company in Canada in a year or get a manager's job without putting in hard work.

I also believe you need to ignore people who are negative in your life. You know these people: the ones who put up walls, who tell you things won't work or who say it can't be done. You probably have encountered many of those people already. They will suck the life out of you. The more negative friends you have, the more negative you'll become.

Getting a "perfect" job in the area that you want and are qualified for within three months might be an unrealistic goal; it will more likely take you longer. But, you have to work at it. Talk to as many people as possible and ask questions to get there. It doesn't matter if you're looking for a full-time or part-time job either – the same principles apply.

Humans are complicated beings with so many different needs, wants, moods, motivators, etc. Spending time to make a list of what it is that you want in your job or career will you help find your way.

I've mentioned it in this book already, but I want to make sure that on your list of that "perfect job" are answers to questions like:

- What kind of environment do you like? Open concept? Private offices? Noisy? Quiet?
- What type of industry? Manufacturing? Banking? Service?
- What type of company? Start-up? Established? Doesn't matter?
- What size of company? Large? Small? Doesn't matter?
- What do you want to wear? (I'm not joking – do you want to wear a business suit, are you more comfortable in jeans, or does it matter to you?)
- How far do you want to commute each day? 30 minutes one way? Less? More?
- What hours do you want to work? Monday to Friday, 9:00-5:00? Days? Evenings? Weekends? More? Less?
- What kind of boss do you want to work for? Do you get along better with males or females or does it matter to you? Do you want a boss who micro-manages or who leaves you alone to do your work?
- What kind of work do you want to be doing? Project work or transactional type work or a combination of both?
- What else is important to you?

There are lots of items that you can have on your list and it may take you a few days or even weeks to come up with it as you think of things that can be added, deleted or changed. If I added it all up, my own list that I did years ago probably took me about five to seven hours over a three week period and had over 50 points on it. Yours might take you more or less time.

Notice that I didn't include "How much am I looking to get paid?" on the list of questions above. The reason I wouldn't suggest including that question is that if you find a position or opportunity that has everything on your list, wouldn't you do whatever it took, including working for free, just to get there? If you knew that an opportunity could get you where you wanted to go, wouldn't you sacrifice as much as you could, including getting paid, if you knew that it could lead to something greater in the future?

The money will come if you find something you truly love because you'll want to keep getting better and better and someone will eventually pay you for your experience, whether it's a company, supplier, your boss, etc. Think of that hockey player who practiced hundreds of hours growing up and not earning a penny because of the love of the game and who ended up getting paid millions of dollars a season when he made it to the NHL.

Remember also that it's your list. If you show your list to someone don't be surprised if they will have some kind of an opinion, either positive or negative, about your list. Don't let any negativity get in the way of what you're looking to do.

I would challenge you to think of your list not only as a one-time event – your list should be updated at least once a year, maybe at the start of each calendar year. Pull out your list and see if the things on there are still applicable. Add, delete or change your list as required. Then compare it to what you're doing in your current role – is your current role meeting at least 95% of the points on your list? If not, maybe it's time to find something else. I'm sure you've heard the expression "Do what you love and the money will follow." If you love what you do, it won't feel like work. Set out to find what you love to do.

Your list will help you start your path to finding your way, but it's also only part one of a two-step process and it requires less work than the second part!

Step two in finding that perfect job is tougher than step one and many people won't even consider it, presumably because it's too much effort and there's no defined end game. (Mind you, most people won't even get to step one. If you've done step one, you're probably only one out of ten job seekers. Of the 10% of the people who may complete step one, my guess is that only 10% of that group will complete step two, which means only one percent of people will do both steps.)

So, step two is this: Now that you have your list, what opportunities are out there that meet 95% or more of your points on your list? It may take some time to think about it. You might come to the realization that being a financial analyst will give you everything you want. Or maybe becoming an entrepreneur like me is the way you want to go. Or maybe becoming a waste collector. It doesn't matter because, after all, it will give you everything you want in your career. It will make you want to get out of bed every morning excited about the prospects of doing what you love every day. Expand your world and have an open mind!

Think about the kinds of opportunities that meet as many of the criteria on your list as possible. As I did, start with the NAICS or SIC codes if you're having trouble thinking of industries that have the kind of role that you're looking for.

Meet people, ask questions and share your list of what you're looking for with people you know. Think of who can give you that opportunity. It's not easy to find the perfect fit. There's no doubt it will take you some time. For me it took me more than six months to find my perfect opportunity. Take your time because, after all, we're talking about your career, right? You don't want to rush it!

When you find that position, you'll have a "eureka" moment and there won't be any stopping you. If someone won't hire you in the position you're looking for right away because of your lack of experience, you will figure out the steps of how to get there, perhaps by volunteering on nights and weekends.

You don't need to have certain letters behind your name or have gone to the most prestigious school to get what you're looking for. All it takes is determination and not being afraid of asking questions or picking up the phone to call someone to get more information, and perhaps a bit of luck. I believe, though, that luck just doesn't happen. That sports superstar didn't just have luck. Yes, they might have been blessed with tremendous ability and skills, but they also practiced every day to keep improving themselves to get to the top of their game. The harder you work, the luckier you get.

Even winning the lottery takes more than just luck – you have to buy a ticket first! You don't need any luck to buy a ticket… just a couple of dollars and spending the time to go out to buy the ticket!

When I had my own eureka moment back in 2004, it was amazing. I had figured out my dream opportunity. For every negative person or objection that someone threw at me as to why it wouldn't work, I had another reason to prove them wrong.

During my process of becoming an entrepreneur, I asked others every question I could think of, even if initially I thought they were stupid questions. Take it from me - no question is too stupid. I found out the answers to anything I didn't know. I thought through how I would deal with issues that would come up. Ask people who have been there. Ask people for their opinion, but remember that you get what you pay for – people's opinions are free and lots of people have opinions about stuff they don't really know or understand!

I have spoken with many people I've met over the years, who have given me both great and lousy advice. Be careful of family members who think they know it all, or friends that pretend to have all the answers. They can be huge negative influencers in your life and may have other reasons for being negative (e.g. maybe their own jobs or careers aren't going well for them). Remember that they're not walking in your shoes. They're not the ones with your list. It's *your* list.

Some of you reading this book will be motivated to take control of your job and career while others will put this book down and not do anything – the choice is yours. What type of person are you?

Take control of your career. It's not the responsibility of your parents, spouse, boyfriend or girlfriend, friend or anyone else. It's yours. If you need guidance, find a coach that you're comfortable with and meet with them to ask them for direction. Sit down and really reflect on what it is that you want. That time that you spend will be invaluable.

I leave you with a few quotes that will hopefully put things into perspective and give you some motivation to go out and get that "perfect" job!

"Whether you think you can or can't, you're right." - Henry Ford

"Whatever the mind of man can conceive and believe, it can achieve." - Napoleon Hill

"Real knowledge is to know the extent of one's ignorance." - Confucius

Oh, and by the way, you are probably wondering what happened to Carlos, Raj and Ann.

The four periodically got together for lunch or dinner after their last meeting about starting up a business.

At the suggestion of Chris, Ann spoke with her manager about the concerns she was having in her job and they began to work better together. Ann was promoted to a management position six months after her manager left the company. She ended up staying with her company for another two years. After that, she became manager of accounting at a larger company and has been there for a few years. She expects to stay in that role for the foreseeable future and enjoys managing people.

Raj found a temporary administrative position at Carlos' company thanks to a recommendation by Carlos. That temporary position became full-time and, eventually, Raj applied internally to a position in the IT area. He then became an IT manager and now supervises eight people in his department. He enjoys the stability and remembers how difficult it was to get there.

Carlos ended up opening up his own IT business. In fact, it's a Canadian success story, and he's enjoying every minute of entrepreneurship.

Chris continued his recruitment business for years, but because he always wanted to get into radio in some form or other, he ended up having his own call-in show on Sunday mornings on a local radio station. His show? "Tales from the Recruiter"

I wish you luck in your job and career search. I've left you with some final tips of things to do when you find your dream job (*Appendix 13*).

Feel free to reach out to me at any time! I will get back to you! And let me know if you have changed your job search process or have had any successes as a result of reading this book.

Get more tips on your job search and updates at www.TalesfromtheRecruiter.com or at www.TorontoJobs.ca!

Marc Belaiche, CPA, CA
(a.k.a. "Chris the Recruiter")
President
TorontoJobs.ca
Marc.Belaiche@TorontoJobs.ca
905-566-5627x2873
866-486-5627x2873

GLOSSARY OF TERMS

Active Job Seeker: An applicant actively looking for a new position and applying to job postings. See also *Passive Candidate.*

Application Form: A series of questions that need to be filled out on a form by a job seeker. The form may require the job seeker to include information such as name, address, work history, salary expectations, etc.

Base Salary: The amount paid to an employee, typically expressed as an annual amount (e.g. $35,000 per year).

Behavioural Interview Questions: A type of interview question that tests a job seeker's reaction to certain conditions that are expected to be a part of the job they are applying for. For example, "What would you do if…" See also *Standard Interview Questions.*

Benefits: Other compensation given by a company to their employees, such as health and dental benefits, car allowance, etc.

Bonus: Additional money given by companies to employees for individual, team, or company-wide performance.

Burdens: Amounts paid by an employment agency for a temporary employee, for example payroll taxes and vacation pay.

Candidate: See *Job Seeker.*

Career Coach: Someone who helps job seekers understand their career aspirations and guides them to find the positions that would meet their objectives

Career Fair: A gathering where job seekers can interact with potential employers.

Career Goals: An idea of the direction a job seeker would like to see their professional career develop. For example, "In five years, I'd like to be a controller."

Chronological Resume: A resume in which a person's accomplishments are listed in order of the time in which they occurred, with the most recent positions showing first, as opposed to a functional resume. See *Appendix 2.*

Company Hierarchy: A chart of the positions in a company relative to each other which shows who reports to whom.

Compensation: The pay (base salary salary or hourly rate) plus benefits that a company gives to an employee in exchange for their work.

Contingency Recruiting Firm: A type of recruiting firm where the client only pays the firm when they have successfully found a candidate. See also *Retained Search Firm*.

Contract Employee: An employee who is working for a company for only a pre-determined amount of time, such as 3 months, 6 months, a year, etc.

Corporate Recruiter: A human resources representative working at a company, other than an employment agency, who is focused on finding suitable candidates for open positions within their organization.

Counter-Offer: When an employee resigns from their position to go to a new company, and their current employer offers them more money or other incentives to stay with the organization instead of leaving.

Cover Letter: A letter written by a job seeker that is attached to a resume which gives additional information about a job seeker that is not covered in their resume, typically one page. See *Appendix 6, 7 and 8*.

Curriculum Vitae (or C.V.): See *Resume*.

Employment Agency: A company that works on behalf of companies to fill vacancies by finding suitable candidates.

Executive Search Firm: A type of recruiting firm that searches for senior level candidates, for example Chief Executive Officers, Chief Financial Officers, etc.

Exit Interview: A series of questions asked by an employer to an employee who has given their resignation.

Extracurricular Activities: Things that a job seeker does which do not impact their work experience.

Full-time Employment: A job opportunity where the total number of hours worked is typically at least 35 hours per week.

Functional Resume: A resume in which a person's accomplishments are listed by their importance to the job, as opposed to a chronological resume. See *Appendix 3*.

Head-hunter: See *Recruiter*.

Hidden Job Market: The available positions in a company or industry that are not publicly advertised.

Informational Interview: A meeting between a job seeker and a professional contact, in order for the job seeker to gather information about a profession, company, or industry.

Internship: A job opportunity that gives a job seeker the chance to be trained in a certain profession; this could be paid or unpaid.

Interview: A question and answer session held between a company and a prospective employee regarding an open position.

Job Advertisements: Positions that are advertised, for example on a job board.

Job Board: A website which lists open job positions and their job descriptions.

Job Description: A detailed look at the roles, responsibilities, and requirements of a particular position.

Job Fairs: A gathering of prospective employers and job seekers. See *Appendix 11* for tips.

Job Offer: An offer of employment by an employer to a job seeker.

Job Seeker: A person currently looking for employment. See also *Candidate*.

Manager: A person in a position of authority in an organization.

Mentor: An experienced person in a company or industry who provides guidance to a newcomer to the field or organization.

Multiple Offers: Offers of employment to one job seeker from two or more employers at the same time.

NAICS: North American Industry Classification System; a list of every industry that organizes businesses by their type of economic activity.

Networking: Meeting with, and getting to know, other professionals. See *Appendix 4*.

Notice Period: The amount of time an employee gives to their employer before they will leave the company when they resign, typically two weeks.

Organizational Chart: A structure showing the relationships between the different positions in a company.

Outplacement: A program, typically paid by an employer for an employee who has been terminated from the company, to help the employee with their resume, interviewing tips and coaching. The program is provided by an outplacement firm.

Outplacement Firm: A company that specializes in providing outplacement services to a terminated employee.

Panel Interview: An interview where one job seeker is questioned by numerous members of a prospective employer at the same time.

Part-Time Employment: A job opportunity where the total number of hours worked in a week is typically less than 35.

Passive Job Seeker: An applicant who is not actively looking for a new position and not necessarily responding to job postings, but would be open to hearing about opportunities if approached. See also *Active Candidate*.

Phone Interview: A series of questions asked by an employer to a job seeker over the phone.

Placement Fee: The cost to an employer for using a recruitment agency to find a suitable candidate for a position.

Probationary Period: An initial period (typically three months) after an employee has started with a company during which the employer can terminate the employee and not have to pay any additional amount to the employee.

Recruiter: A human resources representative who is focused on finding suitable candidates for open positions.

Recruiting Firm: See *Employment Agency*.

Red Flag: Something about the job seeker that might cause concern for a recruiter.

Reference: Someone that can provide information to a prospective employer about a candidate's background, including work experience.

References: A list of contacts (usually two to three) that a hiring company can speak to regarding a job seeker who will be able to describe the job seeker's experience before the company hires the individual. This list is provided by the job seeker to the company.

Reference Check: A process whereby a recruiter or an employer asks references questions about a candidate's work experience.

Referral Bonus: A bonus paid to company employees for referrals which lead to a new hire.

Resignation Letter: A short letter written by an employee to his/her manager when they are quitting their position. Typically no more than one page. See *Appendix 12*.

Resume: An overview, typically two pages, of a person's work experience, skills and qualifications.

Resume Database: A catalogue of resumes maintained by a company or employment agency.

Resume Writer: A person who can help a job seeker prepare or review their resume.

Retained Search Firm: A type of recruiting firm that charges their clients a retainer regardless whether the search firm is able to place a candidate. *See also Contingency Recruiting Firm.*

Retainer: A deposit paid by a company to a recruiting firm to undertake a search for a candidate.

Salary: The monetary compensation paid to an employee for the work done.

Salary Grid: A range of salaries for various positions.

Salary Range: The maximum and minimum salaries paid to the individuals of a given profession or type of position.

Salary Survey: A study of the average salaries earned by job seekers based on experience.

SIC Codes: Standard Industrial Classification. A system for classifying businesses by industry.

Skill Selling: When a recruiter contacts a company to discuss a particular candidate who has a specialized skill or experience.

Staffing Agency: See *Employment Agency*.

Staffing Firm: See *Employment Agency*.

Standard Interview Questions: Basic informational questions asked by a recruiter or company representative to a job seeker, such as salary expectations, work history, career goals, etc. See also *Behavioural Interview Questions*.

Strengths: Skills of an individual that they are able to execute well, for example written or oral communication, multi-tasking, etc.

Supervisor: The person in an organization whom an employee directly reports to.

Temporary Employee: An employee who works at an organization for a pre-arranged short amount of time, such as for three weeks. See also *Contract Employee*.

Temporary Placement: A short-term position.

Temporary Work: A short-term role.

Thank You Letter: A follow-up to an interview in which the candidate has an opportunity to further emphasize their strengths to the interviewer in a letter or email. See *Appendix 9 and 10*.

Video Interview: A series of questions asked by an employer to a job seeker over computer video software, such as Skype (www.skype.com).

Volunteering: An internship that is unpaid.

Weaknesses: Skills of an individual that they are unable to execute as well, for example managing employees or delegating.

APPENDICES

Appendix 1 – Resume Writing Tips

Your resume is the first and most important document for getting the job you want. Some recruiters receive hundreds of resumes per day, so getting your resume to stand out from the rest can be challenging.

Your resume should be a well-organized profile of your qualifications for a career. It should also communicate enough information to an employer to keep them interested.

Here are some suggestions to write an effective resume:

Two pages
Your resume should generally be a maximum of two pages long. Typically, there are not a lot of reasons to go over that.

Write with style
The font size of text throughout the resume should be 12 point and either Times New Roman or Arial style - keep it consistent. Don't alternate between fonts throughout unless the changes are consistent. Use one-inch margins at the top and bottom and sides of your resume. Try to avoid using horizontal or vertical lines, graphics, or shading. Try to avoid overusing italics, scripts and underlined words.

Use effective vocabulary
Define all experiences with as many action words as possible, such as accomplished, delegated, achieved, conducted, coordinated, organized, etc.

Don't get too personal
Your name, address, postal code, telephone number and email address is appropriate to include in your resume. Specific personal information such as age, birthdate, marital status, citizenship, etc. is not important and should not be included in your resume. Also avoid using nicknames.

Objective
Write what you want to do and be specific. Explain in one or two sentences how your abilities will benefit the company or organization for which you are applying at the top of your resume.

Achievements
Show your unique skills and list the most important and relevant skills first.

Work Experience
Most people should use a chronological resume format (see *Appendix 1)*, and not a functional resume format (see *Appendix 2)*. List experience in reverse chronological order; that is, your most recent experience should be listed first.

Include the following information in your resume:
- Title of position
- Name of organization
- Location of work (city, province)
- Dates of employment
- Describe your work responsibilities and list specific accomplishments

Volunteer Experience
List any related volunteer or community experience.

Education
Show your most recent education first and then go back in time, similar to how you show your work experience. Include the years you attended each school and any degree(s) or diploma(s) received.

Interests
List specific interests that will show that you have the skills and attitude needed by the employer.

References
Add a note that you will provide references if needed at the bottom of your resume (e.g. "References available upon request"). This is a standard statement, even though it may be obvious. You don't need to list your references on your resume.

The finished product should look outstanding. Make sure your resume is neat, proofread for spelling errors, and be factually accurate!

Appendix 2 – Sample Resume - Chronological style

BETTY JUNE
Street Address
City, Province, Postal Code
Phone

OBJECTIVE

To work as a part of a team where I can apply my acquired knowledge and abilities and contribute to the company's ongoing success.

QUALIFICATIONS

- Proven experience in customer service and sales
- Able to work independently or as part of a team
- Excellent communication and interpersonal skills
- Responsible, trustworthy, accountable, and hardworking
- Languages: English, French

WORK EXPERIENCE

Operations/Customer Service Manager Trans-Pose Logistics
Mississauga, ON   **2008-Present**
Trans-Pose Logistics is an international company that offers a wide array of transportation services to move freight on clients' schedule.

Responsibilities
- Manage/Supervise drivers
- Dispatching, planning and coordinating daily activities
- Answer phones, receive/deliver faxes and emails, attend meetings, take minutes
- Keep track of attendance and generate month end reports
- Prepare charts, reports, spreadsheets and manage files
- Answer client inquiries

Animator Purple Dollies Day Camp
Mississauga, ON   **2007-2008**
Purple Dollies Day Camp is a private, not-for-profit, charitable organization well-known for its quality programs. Since 1928, Dollies has offered camping, education and recreation programs all year-round for the community and beyond.

Responsibilities:
- Travel to different schools, daycares, day camps
- Teach and interact with students ages 18 months to 14 years old
- Show students live animals such as snakes, lizards, insects, frogs
- Perform a variety of scientific experiments with students
- Play and have fun with kids

Fitness Director Silver Fitness Centre
Mississauga, ON   **2006-2007**
Silver Fitness Centre is the largest fitness centre in Canada by adhering to a simple philosophy of providing highly trained associates, innovative programming and top-notch equipment.

Responsibilities:
- Personalized consultations with clients and personal training
- Educational seminars and corporate wellness development
- Designed and instructed members through aerobic routines
- Booked and planned schedules and appointments
- Applied and enforced rules and regulations of facility
- Performed administrative duties including month end reports

Fitness and Lifestyle Management Advanced Diploma
2004-2005
ABC City College, Toronto, ON

Office Automation Technology Certificate
          2003-2004
Tech Montreal, Montreal, QC
Trained in a one year program

Customer Service Certification
1997

Hospitality Services, Montreal, QC

References available upon request.

Appendix 3 – Sample Resume - Functional Style

TOM JOHNSON
Street Address
City, Province, Postal Code
Phone
Email

OBJECTIVE

Executive Director for a well-established organization in the health care industry.

HIGHLIGHTS

- Proven ability in developing and maintaining long-term client relationships, with several Fortune 500 companies.
- Over 18 years of experience in business development, account management, production and manufacturing.
- Over five years' management experience emphasizing a collaborative yet decisive style.
- Adept at building productive relationships to further the organization's goals.
- Persuasive skills, both written and verbal.

PROFESSIONAL EXPERIENCE

Management

- Achieved a revenue growth from $600K to $1.5M per year within my area of management, while keeping overhead low.
- Planned and adhered to a budget of up to $750K.
- Supervised a staff of 15, involving training, work flow, quality control, conflict resolution, and review processes.
- Directed the acquisition, installation, and maintenance of a 40 workstation system.

Development/Motivation

- Built a large loyal client base through personal attention, quality service, and consistent follow-through.
- Assisted clients in identifying their interests, and motivated them to act accordingly.

- Wrote persuasive letters and documents, frequently influencing decision-makers.
- Involved personnel in goal sharing, resulting in dramatically increased productivity.

WORK HISTORY

2000 - Present Assistant Manager

Pro One Services, Edmonton AB

1995 - 2000 - Office Manager

Vancouver Health, Vancouver BC

EDUCATION

Finance Diploma, Expert College, Winnipeg MB, 1996
B.A., Finance, University of Calgary, Calgary AB, 2000

AFFILIATIONS

Finance Quarterly - Finance group that meets on a monthly basis to discuss changes in finance.

References available upon request.

Appendix 4 – Networking Tips

Networking is an important way to develop contacts. If you can develop a personal relationship with prospects before you pick up the phone to call them, they are more likely to be receptive to a meeting.

Networking is beneficial because you meet people who can introduce you to other decision-makers and it enables you to build a base of referrals and introductions which can be used in the future.

Here are some tips to follow when networking:

Know yourself
Make sure you know yourself, what you want, and what you excel at. This means knowing the direction you are headed for and being able to communicate to others what it is that you have to offer.

Carry your resume with you
Ensure your resume is with you at all times when you are job searching – you never know who you will meet! You can also have business cards printed, usually for a small charge for small quantities.

30 second infomercial
Have a 30 second infomercial ready when you network, describing what you're looking for, your background and anything else relevant.

Create a good first impression
When meeting someone for the first time, start with a warm smile, make eye contact and have a firm handshake. Introduce yourself, ask how you can help them, let the person know what you do and explain that you're looking for a position. Don't forget to thank them.

Conduct informational interviews
An informational interview is a meeting between you, the job seeker, and a professional contact. The purpose of this is for you, the job seeker, to gather information about a profession, company, or industry.

Join professional associations
Membership in a professional association provides you with an ideal networking opportunity. Some associations are geared towards certain industries, so this is a great way to make contacts in your area of interest.

Tales from the Recruiter

Volunteer
Volunteering is a great way to make contacts – you can volunteer to sit on a committee, organize events, provide services, etc. The important thing is to volunteer for something that you are interested in and inspired by. This will lead you to meet other like-minded people.

Keep your network organized
It is important to recognize that each person in your network is valuable, even if the value isn't immediately apparent. Make sure to keep your network organized with contact information, company name, title and any other information you've learned about them. Jot notes on the back of someone's business card after you first meet them to remind you of what you discussed and what you learned about them.

Make real connections with people
Networking is about quality, not quantity – it should be about connecting with people, not just collecting business cards. The goal of networking is not to land you a job, but to build a network of people that you have a meaningful relationship with. This will last much longer, and be more beneficial. Remember, it's not just who you know, it's who knows you.

Don't be afraid to ask for help
People are often flattered that you think they can assist you. Contacts can give you a lot of useful information, such as a referral to a new contact, a tip about a job and information about the industry you're interested in.

Offer to help
Remember, networking isn't just about the end goal of getting a job. It's a give-and-take situation, and sometimes the most beneficial thing you can do is offer to help someone in your network. Helping someone else often helps to build a stronger relationship, and there is a greater likelihood that they'll want to do you a favour in the future, such as giving you information on a job they know you'd be perfect for!

Keep in touch with your network
Keeping in touch doesn't mean every day – this will turn most people off. It means that you should be mindful of the relationship. Next time you read an article that someone in your network might be interested in, send it to them. Who knows what you'll get in return some day?

Appendix 5 - Interviewing Tips

<u>Make a good first impression</u>
Make a positive first impression with everyone you meet. That includes the receptionist or anyone who walks by while you're waiting in the lobby.

<u>Dress appropriately</u>
Play the part – dress appropriately for the position. It is not the best idea to walk into an interview dressed casually when the interviewer is wearing a suit and tie.

<u>Arrive early</u>
Allow yourself extra time for the commute to ensure you arrive on time. If you realize you are going to be late have the courtesy to call the interviewer and let them know.

<u>Sit upright</u>
Don't slouch during the interview - it displays that you are not very interested in the position.

<u>Keep eye contact</u>
Keep eye contact with the interviewer(s). When responding to questions, look the interviewer in the eye with confidence regarding your work experience and past accomplishments.

<u>Listen</u>
Do not cut off the interviewer when they are speaking. Listen to the entire question asked and think before you answer.

<u>Know what position you are targeting</u>
When a recruiter asks what your next ideal position would be, you should never answer with "I will take anything." Recruiters want to know what you want. Don't be vague.

<u>Don't say you know something when you don't</u>
Saying you know something when you don't will hinder your chances at the position. Don't bluff.

<u>Bring extra resumes, a pen and paper</u>
Bringing extra copies of your resume is good for two reasons. First of all, you may have an opportunity to meet with other people at the company.

Secondly, use the resume to refer to as a guide when answering questions. Bring a pen and paper to take notes.

Stay focused
Focus on your achievements. These accomplishments should be related to the position being discussed.

Don't dominate the conversation
Answer the questions of what is asked of you. Do not ramble about other topics.

Don't give the wrong answer
Make sure you listen to the question and take a moment to gather your thoughts before you respond.

Remain positive
Ensure that you are always positive about past employers and avoid any negative comments directed at a previous employer. Make sure to smile.

Let the interviewer know that the position is of interest to you
When the interview is about to conclude, ensure that you have stressed to the interviewer that you are interested in the position.

Interview the interviewer
Have questions ready to ask the interviewer. It gives you a chance to clarify anything the interviewer might have forgotten to mention. Examples of questions you can ask are:

- What is the future potential for the successful candidate?
- What challenges is the department/company currently having?
- How long do you expect the successful candidate to stay in this role?

Do not ask about salary, compensation or benefits in your first interview.

Ask for a business card
Getting a business card will make sure that you have the right contact information for sending them a thank you letter after the interview.

Appendix 6 – Cover Letter Checklist

This section contains a checklist of what should be included when writing an effective cover letter.

- ☐ The contact name and company name are correct.
- ☐ The letter is addressed to an individual, if possible.
- ☐ The letter mentions the position you are applying for and where it was listed.
- ☐ Your personal information (name, address, home phone, cell phone, email) is included and correct.
- ☐ If you have a contact at the company, you have mentioned him or her in the first paragraph.
- ☐ Cover letter is targeted to the position you are applying for.
- ☐ Letter is focused, concise, clear, and well-organized.
- ☐ Use opening phrases like "I am writing in reference to the position you advertised" or "Attached is my resume for your perusal."
- ☐ At the end of the cover letter say a phrase such as "I look forward to hearing from you soon."
- ☐ If you have a gap in your employment history you have explained it in your cover letter.
- ☐ It is printed on good quality paper that matches the font, size and style of your resume. Font is 11 or 12 points and easy to read (Times New Roman or Arial, for example).
- ☐ No spelling or grammatical errors.
- ☐ You have read the cover letter out loud to make sure there aren't any missing words.
- ☐ The letter is a maximum of one page.
- ☐ You have kept a copy for your records.
- ☐ Sign the letter.

Appendix 7 – Cover Letter Template

This is a sample template that you can use for a cover letter.

Your Name and Contact Information

Date

Employer Name and Contact Information (if you have it)

Salutation
Dear Mr./Ms. Last Name, (leave out if you don't have a contact)

First Paragraph
The first paragraph of your letter should include information on why you are writing to the employer. Mention the position you are applying for and where you found the job listing. Include the name of a mutual contact, if you have one.

Middle Paragraph(s)
The next section of your cover letter should describe what you have to offer the employer. Mention specifically how your qualifications match the job you are applying for. Remember, you are interpreting your resume, not repeating it.

Final Paragraph
Conclude your cover letter by thanking the employer for considering you for the position. Include information on how you will follow-up.

Complimentary Close
Respectfully yours, (other examples include: Sincerely, Regards or Thank You)

Signature

Appendix 8 – Cover Letter Sample

JAY EDWARD
Address, City, Province, Postal Code
Phone
Email Address

<date>

Mike Smith, Recruitment Manager
The Admin Office
2369 Main Street
North York, Ontario
M6Z 4K7

Dear Mr. Smith,

I am interested in expanding my professional horizons by seeking new challenges in the area of **accounting.**

While reviewing the enclosed resume, you will find that in addition to a Bachelor of Business in Accounting, I have more than 15 years of hands-on office and accounting expertise. One of my greatest strengths is sustaining a highly productive and efficient workplace. I achieve this by streamlining operations, implementing professional development seminars and establishing a good rapport with both clients and co-workers.

As a team member of your organization, I can provide:
- Efficiency, reliability, accuracy, as well as manage and coordinate daily activities and office workflow, ensuring timely completion of assignments.
- Maturity, honesty and the ability to look at challenges as opportunities, and effectively make sound judgments and decisions.

Mr. Smith, my objective is to establish a time when we can meet to discuss how my experience, professionalism and enthusiasm will add value to your organization. Thank you for your consideration, I look forward to speaking with you soon.

Sincerely,
Jay Edward

Appendix 9 – Thank You Letter Tips

Here are some tips when writing a thank you letter.

1. The thank you letter should be written soon after an interview (within one to two business days). The letter expresses appreciation and thanks the interviewer for their time.
2. View your thank you letter as a sales letter. In other words, you can restate why you want the job, what your qualifications are, how you might make significant contributions, etc.
3. The thank you letter is also the perfect opportunity to discuss anything of importance that your interviewer didn't ask you or that you neglected to answer as thoroughly, or as you would have liked.
4. Remember to proofread. Check for spelling, grammar, typos, etc. If in doubt about the correct names, spellings or titles of your interviewers, call the company to double-check.
5. Send a letter to each person who interviewed you. If you were interviewed by more than one person each interviewer should individually receive a letter of thanks to ensure consistency.

Appendix 10 – Sample Thank You Letter

This is a sample thank you letter you can use.

<date>

Elizabeth Terry
Director, Human Resources
ABC Company
123 Main Street
Victoria, British Columbia
V2C 1A6

Dear Mrs. Terry:

Thank you for taking the time out of your busy schedule to talk to me about the Account Executive position with your organization. I appreciate your time and consideration in interviewing me for this position.

After speaking with you and the group, I believe that I would be a perfect candidate for this position, offering the quick learning and adaptability that is needed for a diversified position. In addition to my enthusiasm for performing well, I would bring the technical and analytical skills necessary to get the job done.

I am very interested in working for you and look forward to hearing from you once the final decisions are made regarding this position. Please feel free to contact me at (include your personal email address) anytime if further information is needed. My cell phone number is (555) 555-5555.

Thank you again for your time and consideration.

Sincerely,
Your Name
Email Address
Address
Phone Number

Appendix 11 – How to Make the Best of Job Fairs

Job fairs are a tremendous way for job seekers to connect with employees, if well-planned and handled properly. Most of the benefits of these shows will result from proper planning, rather than the actual day itself. Here are some tips for job seekers to maximize the benefits at job fairs.

Preparation before the event

1. Be prepared for possible interviews — have answers ready to common questions (e.g. type of position looking for, salary expectations).

2. Prepare questions you want answered before you arrive.

3. Get familiar with the layout of the job fair by reviewing the show materials.

4. Find out what companies will be there and, if/when possible, what positions they are looking to fill. Do research on those companies and positions ahead of time.

5. Plan to go when the event is not as busy so that you can spend more time with employers. Busy/slow times will vary from show to show depending on many factors including the location, times of the show and the amount of advertising done by the organizers. Try to avoid going very late to shows as exhibitors may not be as well-prepared during those times (they may be tired from a long day on their feet).

6. Prepare a 30-second "sales pitch" of your background and what you're looking for that you can recite when you meet with exhibitors.

7. Make a checklist of what exhibitors you want to meet at the show so you can make sure you don't miss any.

8. Find out information about companies who are going to be there to review any positions that might be open ahead of time.

At the job fair

1. Dress professionally, as if you are going for an interview.

2. Have a portfolio or professional case for your resumes.

3. Bring a sufficient supply of resumes and business cards to hand out to selected employers.

4. Only approach companies that can help you — try not to waste exhibitors' time, especially at busy shows.

5. Be polite and gracious to exhibitors and other attendees; don't try to hoard time so that no one else gets an opportunity. Return to the booth later if necessary.

6. Don't grab all the pens, hats, and bags that you can at booths — this will only reduce your appeal to potential employers.

7. Keep your conversations brief and succinct when meeting exhibitors.

8. Attend any relevant sessions that are available — you may be able to pick up some job search, resume writing or career tips.

9. Ask exhibitors for business cards, when appropriate, to allow for follow-up afterwards; however, keep in mind that some exhibitors may not want to give out their business cards. Don't react negatively if they prefer not to provide their card.

10. Look for non-verbal clues when you're speaking with exhibitors to finish up your conversation (e.g. a lineup behind you is forming; the exhibitor seems to be trying to finish the conversation).

11. Wear comfortable shoes, especially for larger shows.

After the event

1. If possible, find out information about companies that interested you and follow-up with those companies.

2. Follow-up on any business cards that you received – send them a thank you note with your resume again if there was an appropriate position you were looking for that was discussed.

Appendix 12 – Sample Resignation Letter

This is a sample resignation letter you can use.

\<date\>

Mary James
Manager, Sales
Widget Sales Company
321 Main Street
Winnipeg, Manitoba
R3C 4T3

Dear Mary:

I am writing to inform you that I will be resigning from my position with Widget Sales Company as accountant as of (last day of work), two weeks from today.

I appreciate the opportunity to have been part of the team here and have appreciated your leadership. I regret any inconvenience that this will cause, and will do my best to have my current projects finished before my last day. I wish you and the company much success.

Sincerely,

(sign here)

Your Name
Email Address
Address
Phone Number

Appendix 13 - Congratulations! You got the Job!

"Congratulations! You've been hired! See you on Monday!" It's exciting when you hear those words, after getting a job you worked so hard to get and you're eager to get started. However, by the time Monday rolls around, you might have the feeling of excitement turn to butterflies. The first day on a job is nothing to worry about. Make sure you follow these steps to get off on the right foot at your new workplace!

- Call your boss the day/Friday before you start the job and let him/her know how excited you are to be starting the new job. It gives your boss a good impression that you're motivated about the position and the company.

- Planning is the key to a good start at a new job. It's a good idea to plan your route to work before your first day. Plan alternate routes in the event there is a lot of traffic or if public transit is delayed. Know where you will park, or where the nearest bus or train stop is, ahead of time. That way you are prepared and will not get flustered. Avoiding commuting problems will allow you to stay relaxed and help you focus on making a good first impression.

- Dress appropriate to the company environment and wear something you feel confident in. If you feel confident inside, your co-workers will notice it and it will help your initial image.

- Try to arrive at your workplace early on your first day. This will give you the chance to properly greet everyone you encounter.

- Enter with a smile and introduce yourself to everyone you meet. Learn people's names and interests so you feel relaxed with them and they feel comfortable with you. Don't be afraid to ask questions, as most people are more than happy to help a new employee out.

- Bring donuts, go out to lunch, or get together with your new co-workers. Not only will it be easier to break the ice, but you will get the chance to get to know your associates. Take the initiative and people will see you as friendly and approachable.

Tales from the Recruiter

- Finally, make sure recruiters know that you have found a new position. It can be very awkward getting a phone call on your cell while sitting at your new desk from a recruiter who is trying to set up an interview with you for a different position.

After that, just be yourself and do what you do best! Show you are eager to work, and continue to get to know your co-workers' habits and interests to make your transition easier and more enjoyable.

TorontoJobs.ca Service Page

The Local Connection for Qualified Candidates!

HOW CAN TORONTOJOBS.CA HELP YOU FIND A JOB?

• Post your Resume at no cost.

• Visit our Career Resource Centre for articles, salary information and more!

• Apply to 100's of current openings.

• Sign up for daily/weekly JobMail Updates.

HOW CAN TORONTOJOBS.CA HELP YOU FILL AN OPEN POSTION?

• Post your position on TorontoJobs.ca.

• Search our Resume Database of over 100,000 qualified candidates!

• Temporary and Permanent Staffing Services.

CONNECT WITH US!

Website: www.TorontoJobs.ca
General Inquiries: info@TorontoJobs.ca
Send your resume to: resumes@TorontoJobs.ca

LOOKING TO ADVERTISE?
Email: sales@TorontoJobs.ca | **Phone:** 905.566.5627